RUDOLF STEINER
ON HIS BOOK
THE PHILOSOPHY OF FREEDOM

Rudolf Steiner
on his book
The Philosophy of Freedom

Selections arranged and annotated
by

Otto Palmer

THE ANTHROPOSOPHIC PRESS

CONTENTS

	Introduction ix
I.	How the Book Came To Be 3
II.	The Book's Aims and Artistic Composition 11
III.	New Thinking 17
IV. ·	The Sphere of Freedom 28
V.	New Willing 32
VI.	New Thinking, New Willing; The Thinking-Will 41
VII.	Transition to the Social Problem 56
VIII.	The Socially Oriented Will 62
IX.	Forces at Work in the Contemporary Scene 70
X.	The Book as a Training Manual 78
XI.	Confrontations 93
XII.	The Book's Christian Substance 102
	Epilogue 111
	Notes 113
	A Partial Bibliography 119
	Collateral Reading 123

Dedicated to
The Community of Free Spirits
for whom Rudolf Steiner wrote.

Motto:

... the thinking that not only thinks other thoughts but thinks them differently than they were thought before.

Anyone interested in looking for them will find the basic principles already enunciated in my Philosophy of freedom.

Introduction

More than seventy years have passed since the first appearance of *The Philosophy of Freedom*. After that, a quarter of a century elapsed before Rudolf Steiner made up his mind to bring out a second edition of the book. "It would have been possible to keep on publishing new editions," he said at the time, "and I don't doubt they would have found a market. But that would just have meant only that *The Philosophy of Freedom* sold well. In the case of my more basic writings I was never interested in having lots of copies floating around the world. My real concern was to have these writings understood and the impulse in them actually working."[1]

Many further editions have been published since these words were spoken. The time now seems ripe to bring together what Rudolf Steiner himself said and wrote by way of furthering an understanding of this book and of the goal he intended it to serve.

No other book Rudolf Steiner wrote was as often and exhaustively discussed by him as *The Philosophy of Freedom*. He not only refers to it, as in the case of others of his writings, to call attention to some particularly interesting matter treated in its pages; he points again and again and yet again, from every imaginable angle, to what he intended this work to accomplish— indeed, to initiate. The reader will see from the chronological listing of Steiner's comments included at the end of this volume that from 1905 until his death in 1925 not a year passed without some discussion of this first work. The list does not pretend to be complete, however. It would have to include many further references to achieve the status of a true archive, but that task can be undertaken at leisure. Meanwhile, the listing in the appended table may be regarded as containing the most basic references.

The Philosophy of Freedom is a path, a method, as anthroposophy itself is—a method leading by philosophic means to the actual experience of a thinking detached from the body-soul makeup. This is a thinking that cannot be allowed to remain mere thought but must instead become experience based on "soul observation" as the subtitle of the book indicates. As such, it is the first stage of supersensible experience. The second is moral intuition, described in the section called "Moral Fantasy."

Experience of the kind referred to offers the only possible means of refuting materialism, both the scientific materialism of the West and the dialectical materialism of the East. They cannot be refuted by pure logic, for in the closed circuit of the thought systems on which they are based both types have built themselves impregnable fortresses. There is not the tiniest loophole through which one might creep to threaten their hold. They can only be countered by the most solid experience, by the actual fact of experiencing the supersensible in the thinking process. One cannot argue about that experience with people unwilling or unable to attain it, anymore than one can argue with a blind man about the light and color that his defective organism keeps him from perceiving. The experience of pure thinking remains a matter of having the "goodwill," as *The Philosophy of Freedom* says, to undertake it.

The shape of the future depends entirely upon how the human race thinks today. The way we think about ourselves conditions what we will become. Angelus Silesius said, "Man, what thou lovest, into that art thou translated. Lovest thou God, God thou becomest, and earth thou becomest, lovest thou earth." Nowadays it is not so much what we love that is the decisive element as what we think. We take on the shape of the image formed by the way we think about ourselves. So we might change the Silesian mystic's saying to "Man, what thou thinkest, into that art thou transformed. Thinkest thou spirit, spirit thou becomest, and beast thou becomest, conceivest thou thyself as a mere body."

The question as to which is right, the materialistic view of man and universe or the spiritual one, is not primarily theoretical; it is a question we must settle with our wills. Do we want man to be a threefold being endowed with body, soul and spirit, or just a body

x

and soul with a few spiritual attributes? Or is a body with a few soul attributes all we really want? It is up to man alone to decide this issue.

A person able to understand this can also see that *The Philosophy of Freedom*, which poses this world historic problem, thereby lifts itself out of the realm of mere theory to take its rightful place among the decisive factors affecting mankind's future evolution, for it becomes the means to a practical rather than a theoretical overcoming of materialism.

This book offers those who study it the possibility of making themselves truly "free spirits." Materialism does just the opposite. It seeks to reduce us to creatures completely determined by heredity and other such influences, hence totally unfree and little better than animals. That is what materialism has set out to do, and let us not deceive ourselves; it can do it.

Anyone anxious to participate in shaping future man into a spiritually threefold being will have to activate his thinking, to set himself inwardly in motion. Following a path means moving one's feet, not standing still. If one cannot rouse oneself to do this, one resembles a person who studies a map carefully and knows exactly where the path goes, but never starts out to travel it. The map is all that interests him.

The Philosophy of Freedom can, of course, be taken just this way; what would become of freedom were it otherwise?

Nevertheless, to read it that way means taking a more theoretical approach to the study of the path Steiner opened up. That is perfectly justified within certain limits. But there is a danger in it—the danger of becoming too much involved in following up the quotes from Spinoza, Fichte, Hamerling and the various others and making them more of an object of study than is at all necessary for a grasp of *The Philosophy of Freedom*. Such a procedure is quite proper, however, in the case of Steiner's book *The Riddles of Philosophy*[2] because of that book's more historical character.

The quotations included in *The Philosophy of Freedom* were put there for a quite different purpose. That purpose stands out clearly if we leave out the names of the philosophers quoted and consider their thoughts alone, a procedure that changes nothing of consequence in the structure of the book. Then these thoughts serve partly as an obstacle course for the strengthening of our own thinking, partly as prods to stimulate us to reach out for new ideas, and partly as fences to keep our thoughts from straying off in wrong directions. These various goals are fully served by the extent of Steiner's quoting, a fact that relieved him of the necessity of coming to grips within the confines of this book with contemporary developments of philosophic thought. As he said, "There is no need to deal with them in a book with the particular purpose I intended this to serve." These words were followed by a reference to *The Riddles of Philosophy*, which does deal fully with them.

If one responds, as suggested above, to the tutelage the quotes provide, one begins to notice that the thoughts presented in this book are not arranged in a set abstract logical sequence, but instead conduce to a thought dynamics, a veritable thought eurythmy. What we have here is philosophy as an art of thinking.

A person engaging in this dynamic mode of thinking has to activate his will, which gives rise to the "thinking will" that Rudolf Steiner refers to again and again as so essential. Once the reader succeeds in setting this thinking will in motion it is only a question of how far he can develop it, for there are no limits to its possible intensifying.

So he launches out on the path that Rudolf Steiner cleared for him. Quotes to be found in the following pages indicate the importance that Steiner attached to this path as one—though not the only one—that can be taken.

Travelling this path leads to two significant encounters. One is with oneself, with one's own being. The other is with the true essence of thinking. In these two encounters a man experiences himself within thought's very being. This makes him an individual whose life is lived in a pendulum-swing between knowledge that is common property, and his own, fully individual, moral intuitions. Put another way, he learns to transform ideas into ideals. The idea of freedom is a free gift offered him but it is up to him to make this idea activate his will.

If he does so, the idea becomes an ideal.

When he enters thus into possession of his individuality at the point of its origin in the supersensible, he has used every aid that philosophical means can offer him to develop the consciousness soul. As many of his statements show, Rudolf Steiner sees the individual, and the morality issuing from and based upon individuality, as the foundation upon which human society is built.

A person who lifts himself to a truly individual level in the sense of *The Philosophy of Freedom* has, by the same token, developed the capacity to find the concepts and ideas that belong to the phenomena with which the surrounding world confronts him. He lifts himself toward the ideal of the "free spirit" and works to make it a reality.

His efforts in this direction bring forth yet another kind of harvest. He develops an organ, intuition, that not only enables him to have ideas of his own, but to absorb those of others as though they were his. He is thus able to blot out his own world of ideas in order to let another's light up in him. So he comes to understand his fellowman and to develop into a social being.

This enables him to advance from the stage of the consciousness soul in which individualism reaches its highest development, to that of spirit self, which is alone capable of finding solutions to the large and small problems of community life.[3]

We now turn to a discussion of the most important works of other authors on *The Philosophy of Freedom*.

In this connection Carl Unger deserves to be mentioned first. The regard Rudolf Steiner had for Unger's work can be gauged by a remark he made in a lecture entitled *Philosophy and Anthroposophy*.[4] We quote it here at considerable length not only because his words characterize Unger's work; they also set up significant guidelines for anthroposophical work in general.

> The scientist of today is totally unaware of the fact that in the last analysis a truly scholarly spirit has to be based on a thorough-going development of the art of thinking so that this may serve as a solid ground for grasping reality. You will feel, as you hear me say this,

what a blessing it is to see efforts being made in the Anthroposophical Society to work in an absolutely ideal way toward the goal of establishing epistemological principles. The fact that, here in Stuttgart, we have in Dr. Carl Unger an extraordinarily outstanding worker in this field can be regarded as a truly beneficial element in our movement. For the real depths of this movement will not make themselves felt in the world just because there are people in it who want to listen to accounts of supersensible worlds. Its success will rather be due to those who patiently develop a technique of thinking that provides a solid foundation for really successful work, an inner scaffolding for activity in the higher world.

The Philosophy of Freedom was implicit in Unger's thinking, as everything he wrote demonstrates. His final book was *The Language of the Consciousness Soul*[5] a treatise on the guidelines given the Anthroposophical Society by Rudolf Steiner after the Christmas Conference. Although Unger does not mention *The Philosophy of Freedom* until he discusses Guidelines 109-111, it is implicit in everything he says up to that point.

Guideline 109: "To become truly aware of Michael's activity within the cosmic whole is to set the riddle of human freedom in cosmic perspective and thus to solve it, insofar as its solution is a necessity to earthly man."

Guideline 110: "For freedom is an actuality, the immediate possession of every human being who is a true man of his time. Nobody can say that there is no such thing as freedom without denying a perfectly patent fact. But the possession of freedom could seem to run counter to the rule of cosmic order. Such a thought evaporates, however, as one contemplates Michael's mission in the cosmos."

Guideline 111: "My *Philosophy of Freedom* demonstrates the fact of freedom as a content of modern human consciousness. The account of the Michael mission given here tells the story of freedom's cosmic origin and development."

From this point on, Unger constantly quotes from and discusses *The Philosophy of Freedom*. He entitles Section 52 of his commentary "The Michael Aspect of *The Philosophy of Freedom*."

Further commentaries by Büchenbacher, Leiste, Hiebel,

Stockmeyer, Witzenmann and others are listed among the references at the end of this volume.

The statement is made in *An Outline of Occult Science*[6] that "these books [*The Theory of Knowledge Based on Goethe's World Conception*[7] and *The Philosophy of Freedom*] occupy an important middle position between knowledge of the sense world and that of the spirit. They make available what thinking can attain to when it lifts itself above the level of sense observation but stops short of engaging in spiritual research. A person who lets these books work upon his whole being already stands in the spiritual world; he perceives it, however, as a world of thought." A thinking schooled in *The Philosophy of Freedom* and working along the lines of the ideas it stimulates knows exactly what this statement means.

When a person confronts the sense world he is overwhelmed by the onrush of impressions and can hold his own against them only by working his way through to the concepts that belong with and complete them. Percepts exist without his doing, but he has to find the concepts that belong to these.

Thinking is discovered to be a "higher percept" among percepts, for in this case the object of observation and the product of thought are qualitatively identical. Thinking lays hold upon itself in the thinker; the thinker lays hold upon himself in thinking. We are concerned here neither with given facts nor yet with questions remaining to be answered. Instead, everything is pure activity, the activity of thinking on the one hand, the thinker's activity on the other, both laying hold on their own being as they act. Here we have a thought world wholly contained and self-containing.

In this thought world man lives in two realms of reality: that of thinking and that of his own ego-being. His life in the world of thought is what gives him this double nature. It separates him from everything about him, yet also serves as the means of his connection with it, for it is thinking that enables him to grasp the inner aspect of phenomena. The thought world thus enables him to develop all the thoughts and ideas that he needs for an understanding of the sense world.

Anthroposophy, which makes it first appearance in the form of ideas, works in this thought realm on those ideas and concepts which the spiritual investigator develops by means of his spiritual perception and for its furtherance. To the extent that he communicates them to his fellowmen they form a body of a priori facts lacking the factor of perceptibility.

Thus, on the one hand, man finds himself standing in the sense world as in one half of reality, lacking the concepts needed to complete it. He lives in a self-contained world of thought that embraces his concepts and perceptions. When both factors are taken hold of by an energized thinking, observation and intuition merge and are one. On the other hand, man is the recipient of ideas that come to him from the spiritual world, and with these he stands in the other half of reality, which the spiritual world constitutes. What he lacks here is the corresponding percepts. The purpose of spiritual schooling is to guide him to them.

In the lecture quoted above, Steiner describes the situation in which he found himself within the Theosophical Society:

> A person was by no means judged by what he contributed. Instead he was fitted into stereotypes of certain pet notions and phrases.... No one really cared what I was saying and publishing. Of course the members read it, but reading is not the same thing as understanding.... They took what I offered, not as something issuing from my mouth or written in my books, but rather as what this one thought "mystical," that one "theosophical," another something else again.... It was not a particularly appealing or ideal situation in which to bring out a new edition of *The Philosophy of Freedom*.[8]

Here we are being shown an incapacity to enter into the thoughts and ideas of other people, a habitual connecting of certain terms with certain concepts. Habits of this kind get in the way of understanding others' thinking. *The Philosophy of Freedom* has among its many goals that of freeing the reader from fixed thinking habits. If one allows oneself to be guided by the book and enters into the patterns of movement generated by the thoughts it develops, one can reach a capacity to form absolutely exact concepts.

But this alone is not enough. Even if one is able, for example, to think the concept "etheric body" as Steiner would, picturing it not just as attenuated matter or, in other words, conceiving it as something physical, this concept, like many another, is only too apt to remain an isolated one without relationship to others in an organic whole. One has a handful of parts and pieces but the spiritual link is missing. The thinking will is alone able to supply this link, assigning separate concepts and ideas their place of belonging in the total thought sphere.

Steiner has repeatedly emphasized the importance of the thinking will, not only for individuals pursuing occult training but for the advancement of the whole human race.

Considering the danger that *The Philosophy of Freedom* runs of being put in the same category as other philosophies, I feel obligated to assemble Steiner's many and varied comments on this book. Academic philosophy shows a certain wise instinct in ignoring it, for in a sense it represents the end of the road for philosophy and the beginning of something that is wholly new. The book sets forth clearly indeed the philosophic goals still to be achieved.

My sense of obligation outweighs my concern lest this volume present another danger, that is, that the reader will rest content with familiarizing himself with Steiner's comments and use this as an excuse for not developing his own thinking will. This is a risk that will have to be taken.

If one decides to go ahead and undertake the task of assembling and editing what Steiner had to say about his *Philosophy of Freedom,* one finds oneself confronting enormous difficulties.

For one thing, the wealth of writings and lectures is so great that years are bound to pass before one has assembled all the relevant material. The editor has deliberately contented himself with making just a small beginning at that task, aware that even this much was possible only because of work previously done by others.[9] It is to be hoped that still other workers will carry the task through to completion.

A further difficulty is that of deciding where to begin and where to end quoted passages, since these are almost never rounded statements that can stand by themselves. One is, of course, tempted to include every word with any bearing on the subject but to do that would mean allowing this volume to grow to undesirable proportions.

Furthermore, one cannot simply arrange the quotations in chronological order, suitable though such an arrangement is in the case of the chronological table appended at the end. The material at hand has to be presented in some sort of topical arrangement so we settled on the one that follows. Quite aside from all the alternatives that existed in the matter of thematic grouping, however, questions still remained as to the allocation under various headings of passages to be quoted, for it was found that every quotation fitted equally well into some other category. No decision made on this score was really inevitable; some other would have suited just as well. That lay in the nature of the material dealt with, and since there were no perfectly obvious, objective solutions, one had to make arbitrary choices, as has been done here.

The first section of this book presents a short prologue. In it are discussed Steiner's doctoral dissertation, *Human Consciousness Comes to Terms with Itself* (later published with the title *Truth and Science*), submitted to Heinrich von Stein at the University of Rostock, and a letter of Steiner to Rosa Mayreder, surely one of the most touching documents ever to issue from his pen. A quotation from his autobiography is included that throws light on the part Rosa Mayreder played in the development of the theme of freedom.

Let us put what Steiner says in this letter in context with the following remarks of his. "I had the feeling that I was setting down thoughts that the spiritual world had given me up to the time of my thirtieth year," [10] and "This is in no sense a personal work." [11] We do not hesitate to call attention to this seeming contradiction, which will serve as a stimulus to the thinking of the well-disposed, though it affords ill-wishers an unearned triumph.

Finally, this section describes the history of the book from the viewpoint of its author as he surveys it thirty years after its first appearance.

Was it necessary to assign a special chapter to the book's goals and purposes? Indeed it was! As one carries out this survey one finds a great variety of aspects receiving emphasis as the years went by. Then, some attention had to be paid to the book's artistic composition. The sections entitled "New Thinking" and "New Willing (moral fantasy)" touch on the very core of the book and lead over into the Stuttgart lecture of February 6, 1923, entitled "New Thinking, New Willing," which is reproduced here almost in its entirety. What makes its appearance as ethical individualism in the new willing described there is examined in the following section from its social aspect. Between the sections on thinking and willing are inserted Steiner's sharply delineated comments on "The Sphere of Freedom."

It is surely fitting to point out in connection with the latter section that the impulse to freedom is an essential aspect of mankind's task in the fifth post-Atlantean period. This is the basic theme of the lecture, *Episodische Betractung zum Erscheinen der Neuauflage der Philosophie der Freiheit* and we regret having to omit it here.[12] It is certainly the most important and comprehensive commentary Rudolf Steiner ever offered on this subject.

The section which examines *The Philosophy of Freedom* as "A Book of Exercises" is allotted a considerable share of pages. Three different phases stand out distinctly. Around 1907, the book's relationship to Rosicrucian disciplines is stressed; in 1910, its contributions to the anthroposophical path; after the appearance of the second edition in 1918, the emphasis is on the task of lifting the scientific thinking that has served as a schooling for all mankind to the level of a spiritual-scientific means of understanding the universe.

There follow some refutations of critics, of people with differing viewpoints and of enemies. After Steiner's extremely vigorous repelling of attacks by exponents of traditional religious standpoints, it must seem the more surprising to find the last section speaking of the "Pauline" character of this theory of knowledge and to see it shining out at the end as a book of redemptive practices in the pursuit of knowledge.

The longer and more intensively one concerns oneself with the material on which this book is based, the more inclined one is to entitle it "Rudolf Steiner Courts Understanding for his Philosophy of Freedom."

Otto Palmer

Wolfhalden, July 11, 1964

RUDOLF STEINER
ON HIS BOOK
THE PHILOSOPHY OF FREEDOM

CHAPTER I

How The Book Came To Be

As he looked back over his life, Rudolf Steiner found *The Philosophy of Freedom* playing a very decisive role in it. He began concerning himself with the problems the book deals with when, as a young man of nineteen, he entered the Technical High School in Vienna and applied himself to the study of philosophy, among a number of other subjects. In Chapter Three of his autobiography he says:

> As time went on, the life of thinking came to seem to me a reflection in the physical man of what the soul experiences in the spiritual world. Thought-experience meant living in a reality so palpable as to make any questioning of it absurd. But the world of the senses was by no means so real. It is there, to be sure, but one cannot grasp it as immediately as one does one's thoughts. Elements or beings can be working behind its facade. Yet it is the world man finds himself set down in. So the question arose: Is this physical world full reality? When a person develops thoughts about it which he derives from within and applies to its illumination, is he bringing a quite alien element to bear on it? This would not seem to accord at all with his actual experience as he confronts the sense world and penetrates it by means of thinking. Thoughts seem rather to be the medium through which the sense world expresses its own nature. The pursuit of this train of thought occupied a significant place in my inner life at that period.[1]

Here we glimpse the book in embryo.

The same chapter of Steiner's autobiography describes the degree of success this pursuit of knowledge had. "I was developing a state of mind that allowed me to feel capable of defending my view of the spiritual world before the forum of scientific thinking. I was twenty-two at the time these experiences were occupying me."[2]

3

While coming to grips with the philosophy of pessimism, of which his friend Mme. delle Grazie was an adherent, Steiner addressed a piece of writing to her which he called "Nature and Our Ideals." He says of it that it contained the seeds of *The Philosophy of Freedom.* He quotes it at length in Chapter VII of his autobiography, thereby calling attention to the early stages of an evolutionary process that had progressed far enough for him to make a first written statement of it. At the end of Chapter VIII we read:

> At the age of twenty-seven, then, I was beset by questions and riddles related to external aspects of human life, whereas the nature of the soul had all the while been revealing itself to my inner perception in ever more clearly delineated forms as a world for itself. In all spiritual work I put my sole reliance on its contemplation. And this work tended increasingly in a direction that led, several years later, to my writing *The Philosophy of Freedom.*[3]

A further reference to the author's time of life is found in Chapter XVI:

> I can certainly say that the world of the senses had a shadowy, pictorial aspect in my experiencing of it. It passed in review before my soul like a series of pictures, whereas my connection with the spiritual world was absolutely real and genuine. It was in Weimar, in the early 'nineties, that I felt this most keenly. At that time I was giving *The Philosophy of Freedom* its final touches. I felt that I was setting down in it the thoughts the spiritual world had given me up to the time of my thirtieth year. What had come from the outer world merely provided the stimulus.[4]

Steiner was thirty-three when the book appeared in 1894. It is therefore accurate to say that the germinating, ripening, writing and publishing of *The Philosophy of Freedom* spanned a fourteen year period of the author's life, from his nineteenth to his thirty-third year.

Rosa Mayreder was the outstanding personality who did most to further the book's evolution:

> This was the period during which *The Philosophy of Freedom* was taking ever clearer shape within me. Rosa Mayreder was the person with whom I talked most about it as the book developed. She relieved

4

me of some of the inner loneliness in which I lived. Her goal was that of perceiving human personality in all its immediacy, whereas my interest lay in exploring the cosmic panorama which this personality comes to seek when organs of spiritual vision awaken in the soul's depths. Many a bridge was found between the two approaches, and in later life I often recalled with warmest gratitude memories of walks that Rosa Mayreder and I took through glorious Alpine forests, talking the while about what freedom really meant. [5]

This was Steiner's memory of it. But we also have another record, set down just after the book appeared, in the form of a letter from Steiner to Rosa Mayreder, dated November 1894:

Most esteemed and gracious lady!

The words you have written me about my *Philosophy of Freedom* are very *important* to me. I prize in you, among many other qualities, the modernity of your artistic feeling. You have the ability to look at life in the only way it can be viewed in the present era. You are one of that community of "free spirits" of which we dream. I wanted to present you with a real book in this "freedom philosophy" of mine. Your feeling that it measures up to this goal in some degree affords me the greatest reassurance and satisfaction I could have hoped for. I know the exact place where my book belongs in the current of present-day spiritual developments and can point out the exact spot where it carries Nietzsche's line of thinking further. I can make the calm statement that it expresses ideas that are missing in the work of Nietzsche. I confess to my friends—but to them alone—that the fact that Nietzsche can never read my book now pains me. He would have seen it for just what it is: personal experience in every single sentence. But I must tell you that if you had rejected my book it would have caused me incomparable distress. You say that the book is too short, that every chapter has the makings of a book in it. To the extent that you mean this objectively, I can only agree. My reason for writing it as I did, however, was purely subjective. I was not setting forth a doctrine, but simply recording inner experiences through which I had actually passed. And I reported them just as I experienced them. Everything in my book is written from this personal angle, even to the shaping of the thoughts it contains. A theoretical writer could cover more territory, and there was a time when I might have done so. But my purpose was to write a biographical account of how one human soul made the difficult ascent to freedom. In such an ascent one cannot spare any attention to others in the party as they try to negotiate cliffs and precipices, so preoccupied is one with getting up and over them oneself. One's longing to reach the goal is too keen to consider stopping and pointing out the easiest way ahead to other climbers. And I believe I would have fallen had I attempted any such thing. I found my own way up as best I could, and then, later on, described the route that I had taken. Afterwards, I could have found a hundred other different ascent-routes that other climbers might have followed. But at the time I had no desire to write about any of these alternative paths. My method of getting over many a chasm was an individual one, deliberately singled out to be such. I struggled through thickets in a way peculiar to myself alone. And only when one reaches the goal does one realize that one has actually made it. Perhaps the time for handing on theory in a matter like this is already over. Philosophy, except where it is real, individual experience, holds scarcely any further interest for me....[6]

We can also assign to the rubric of help received from other people the strange meetings Steiner describes in Chapter XX of his autobiography. Their strangeness lay in the fact that he never met in the flesh either of the two personalities whose post-mortem influence upon him was so strong. He says:

...My contact with these two souls was a source of strength to me in writing my *Philosophy of Freedom*. What I was trying to set down was, firstly, the outcome of my philosophical thinking during the 'eighties, and secondly, that of my concrete, *general* experience of the spiritual world. My efforts were strengthened by participating in the spiritual experience of the two souls referred to. I witnessed in them the kind of ascent which the soul owes to having had a scientific outlook, and I saw at the same time what fear noble souls like these have of entering into the will-aspect of that point of view. These souls shrank from its ethical consequences.

In my *Philosophy of Freedom* I therefore sought for the force that leads from the ethically neutral world of scientific concepts into the world of moral impulses. I tried to show how a person who, as a result of living in ideas based on material existence rather than still being poured into him from a spiritual source, recognizes himself to be a self-sustained, spiritually endowed nature, can also develop out of his own being an intuitive capacity for experience in the moral sphere.

For this reason, moral ideas light up in the form of individual ethical impulses in persons who have attained to freedom just as scientific ideas do in the contemplation of nature.[7]

We may say, then, that *The Philosophy of Freedom* owes its development in part to thoughts bestowed by the spiritual world, to the unique, warmly human participation of Rosa Mayreder, and to Steiner's experience of the post-mortem life of two friends in the spirit whom he had never encountered on the earth.

       *   *   *

The doctoral thesis written by Steiner for Heinrich von Stein at the University of Rostock must also be listed as a contribution to the book's process of becoming. It was called "Human Consciousness Comes to Terms with Itself." We find the following comment on it in Steiner's autobiography:

> Von Stein was a person of quiet bearing, well along in years, with kindly eyes that seemed both gentle and penetrating as they watched over the progress of his students. Every sentence he spoke was characterized by the cool tone of the philosophic mind. That was how he appeared to me from the first, when I visited him before my examination. He said, "Your dissertation is not quite as required. It is obviously not written under professorial guidance but its content is such that I accept it gladly."[8]

Despite the wise insight with which Heinrich von Stein treated him, Steiner realized that it behooved him to exercise a little caution. He pictures the situation in a lecture given in 1919:

> The whole development of the concepts I had in the field of epistemology culminates in the last two pages of my book *Truth and Science,* where I show that man is the scene of action for cosmic deeds that take place in him, and that what he does takes place in conjunction with the cosmos, from outside rather than from inside himself. These last two pages are the most important part of my *Truth and Science.* Because they are the most important and weighty, because they deal most intensively with what needs changing in the modern outlook, I had to wait to write them in their present form until after this little book, which originally served as my doctoral dissertation, had been accepted. The last two pages were missing from it as a dissertation, for science could hardly be expected to draw consequences from it that would have to mean changes in its whole

outlook. The epistemological groundwork laid in the dissertation was a comparatively innocuous, objective philosophical train of ideas. But what followed from it was something that could be added only at a later date when the book was printed.[9]

If we interest ourselves in the number of pages Steiner devotes in his autobiography to discussing *The Philosophy of Freedom*, we see that it stretches from page 143 in Chapter VIII to page 336 in Chapter XXIII. The most comprehensive exposition of the content of ideas in the book is found in Chapter X. We quote only the beginning and the end of that chapter here:

When I look back over the course of my life, its first three decades seem to me to form a unit by themselves. After that I went to Weimar, where I worked for almost seven years in the Goethe-Schiller Archives. I look back on the time spent in Vienna between the first journey to Weimar described above and my later move to Goethe's city as the period that brought to a certain conclusion what I had been inwardly striving toward up to that moment. This brought me to the point of starting preliminary work on my *Philosophy of Freedom.*

The fact that the sense world was not true reality to me played a vital role among the ideas through which my convictions found expression at that time. In my published writings of the period I kept emphasizing that the human soul shows itself in its actual reality when it engages in a thinking that is not based on the world of the senses but rather transcends the level of sense perception in free-ranging activity. I pictured this 'sense-free' thinking as the element that makes the soul at home in the spiritual being of the world....[10]

I wanted to show that a person who rejects sense-free thinking as a purely spiritual element in man can never grasp what freedom is, but that one instantly understands it when one grasps the reality of sense-free thought.

Here too, I was less concerned at that time with describing the purely spiritual world in which man experiences moral intuitions than with stressing the spiritual nature of these intuitions themselves. Had it been the reverse, I would have had to begin the chapter on moral fantasy in my *Philosophy of Freedom* as follows. "The free spirit acts in accordance with his impulses, that is, with intuitions experienced by him in the purely spiritual world in which he lives remote from nature but unaware of that spiritual world in his ordinary consciousness." But at that time my concern was simply to demonstrate the purely spiritual nature of moral intuitions. So I pointed out the fact that these intuitions exist in the totality of man's world of ideas and therefore said, "The free spirit acts on his impulses, i.e., out of intuitions which thinking selects from the total content of his world of ideas." A person who is not taking the spiritual world into account and would therefore not set down the first sentence could not fully subscribe to the second either. Statements along the lines of the first sentence are, however, to be found in plenty in my *Philosophy of Freedom*, as, for instance, where it states that the highest stage of human life is conceptual thinking without reference to any specific content of perception. We determine the content of a concept purely intuitively, by resort to the ideal realm. Concepts of this kind are not based on specific percepts—meaning here, sense perceptible percepts. If, at that time, I had wanted to write about the spiritual world rather than limit myself to pointing out the spiritual nature of moral intuitions, I would have had to include a discussion of the difference between sense perception and spiritual perception. But my only concern then was to emphasize the non-sense based nature of moral intuitions.

My world of ideas was moving in this direction as the first epoch of my life drew to a close at the age of thirty and the Weimar period began. [11]

We see from these passages that the book's development coincides with the fourth seven-year period of Steiner's life. It was conceived before that period began and published after its completion.

One of the copies of the first edition contains the following lines written in by Steiner:

> Eternal becoming in thinking
> Every step a deepening
> Overcoming the surface,
> Penetrating the depths. [12]

*   *   *

And now a comment on the following statement by Steiner, taken from Chapter XVIII of his autobiography: "I first became acquainted with Nietzsche's writings in 1889. The ideas expressed by me in *The Philosophy of Freedom* were not in the least influenced by his." [13]

9

Steiner's attitude toward Nietzsche can be gathered from the letter to Rosa Mayreder quoted earlier in this section. To make it still clearer, let us quote from another letter, this time to Pauline Specht, that throws light on the matter. In it, Steiner comments on Nietzsche's "Antichrist," which had just been published. He was already familiar with the book, having read it in manuscript. He goes on to say:

> I consider Nietzsche's breakdown one of the worst evils that could have befallen us in our present-day concern with science. Had Nietzsche remained mentally balanced, we would never have witnessed the revolting Nietzsche-craze that meets our gaze wherever we look. That would, of course, have meant having fewer readers who understood him by comparison with the many he now has who, far from furthering any real understanding of him, actually stand in the way of it.
>
> I feel his illness particularly painfully because I am firmly convinced that my *Philosophy of Freedom* would not have gone unnoticed by him. He would have seen that it carried to a further point many questions he left unanswered. He would surely have agreed that his view of morality, his "immoralism," is finally resolved in my *Philosophy of Freedom*, and that when his "moral instincts" are properly sublimated and traced back to their origin, they turn out to be what I have called "moral fantasy." The chapter on moral fantasy in my *Philosophy of Freedom* is just what is missing from Nietzsche's "Genealogy of Morality" in spite of the fact that the book's whole content trends toward it. His "Antichrist" is simply added proof that I am right in this conviction. [14]

We encounter the same view again where Steiner mentions the French philosopher Lichtenberger (cf. the section of this book entitled "Confrontations").

CHAPTER II

The Book's Aims and Artistic Composition

"When a person is charged by his karma with establishing anthroposophy in Central Europe, something must live in this anthroposophy of Goethe's conviction that the element that is the lifeblood of art is also the element of truth, that the element that comes to expression in painting, sculpture and even architecture must also live in truth's thought structure. Indeed, it must be stated, as I tried to do in the first chapter of my *Philosophy of Freedom*, the chapter now put at the end of the new edition, that the philosopher, the founder of a new world conception, has to be an artist in the way he deals with concepts. This image of the conceptual artist is not the usually accepted one, but it is the one I had to base my book on. Everything in it is born of one and the same spirit."[1]

Such is the description Steiner gives of the artistic element permeating *The Philosophy of Freedom*. He says:

Life is made up of many different realms, and every one of them calls for a different kind of scientific approach. But life itself is a unity, and to the extent that science devotes itself to exploring separate areas it loses sight of the living oneness of the cosmos. We must have a science concerned with discovering in the separate scientific fields elements capable of leading us back again to that living wholeness. Investigators in special scientific fields use the facts they discover to build up a picture of the world and its workings. This book has a philosophic goal: that of making science itself alive and organic. The single sciences are only preparatory steps toward the science we are envisioning here.

A similar situation exists in the art realm. A composer works according to the rules of composition. Music theory is a body of knowledge that one must have acquired before starting to compose, and in composing, the laws of composition are made to serve life, to

11

create something absolutely real. Philosophy is an art in exactly the same sense. Real philosophers have always been conceptual artists. The ideas of humankind were the artistic medium in which they worked, and in their hands scientific method became artistic technique. This endows abstract thinking with concrete individual life; ideas become living forces. When this happens, it means not merely knowing about things but transforming knowledge into a real, self-controlling organism, and our true, active consciousness lifts itself above the level of a merely passive taking-in of facts.

My book addresses itself mainly to the question of how philosophy deals as an art with the subject of human freedom, what the nature of freedom really is, and whether we already possess it or can develop it.[2]

If someone were to ask what constitutes the artistic element in the book, we might answer that the thoughts in it do not follow one another in formal, abstract logical sequence; that would have made the book pedestrian. Instead, they are all dynamic movement. Concepts and ideas spring to life, attract and repel each other, conflict with and thus hinder or harmonize and thus further one another, until their liveliness reaches a peak in the chapters "The Idea of Freedom" and "Moral Fantasy," gradually settling down thereafter. This peak comes of the confluence of the various themes, each of which had previously been handled by itself.

In the first section called "Knowledge of Freedom," the reader is shown that concepts and percepts are active factors, and observation and intuition the functions carried out by them. In Chapter IX we find that at a certain level the two factors as well as the functions they exercise are completely merged. This fact, ascertained by soul observation, lies at the root of the view of drives and motives underlying human action that the book develops. Studying them in detail leads to the further discovery that drives and motives too coincide at their highest level. In this merging, in the sphere of knowledge, of concept and percept, intuition and observation, and of drive and motive in the moral sphere, the drama of thinking arrives at its denouement. Now moral fantasy, a wholly new phenomenon, appears on the scene, and though fantasy is ordinarily thought of as the source from which artistic creation issues, here it is shown to be the wellspring that gives rise to moral action.

Now let us look ahead a little (cf. Section II) to comments Steiner made in reply to Eduard von Hartmann's criticism. They show us that *The Philosophy of Freedom* was not intended to champion a one-sided viewpoint. It keeps shifting dynamically from one way of looking at things to another, in continuous movement around a single, common center. All these differing approaches talk together, carrying on a cosmic conversation. This makes the book a work of art from first to last. It was meant to be a shared exercise, not in theoretical thinking but in living experience.

This book, in which the various elements of knowledge and morality are harmonized and differing standpoints unified, is itself the product of experiencing the harmony between goodness, truth and beauty, as the autobiography relates:

> At that period I came to see that genuine knowledge, the reflected shining of the spiritual in art and man's moral will form a single whole. I had to recognize in human personality a central core that links it directly with the world's most fundamental being. Man's will issues from this core, and his willing is free when the clear light of the spirit is at work in it. Then he acts in harmony with the spirituality of the cosmos as it creates, not out of necessity but simply living out its own creative nature. Here, in this central core of man, are born his goals of action, springing from "moral intuitions" rather than from some obscure impulse or other, intuitions as clear and transparent as the clearest thoughts. I wanted my contemplation of free willing to reveal to me the spirit that gives the human individual real existence in the cosmos. I wanted feeling-perception of the truly beautiful to show the spirit at work in man when he acts on the physical plane in such a way that his own being does not just express itself spiritually in free deeds, but so that this spiritual being that he is flows out into a world created by the spirit but not a direct revelation of it. I wanted, in contemplating truth, to *experience* the spirit, revealed in all the immediacy of its own being—the spirit spiritually reflected in moral action, the guide of artistic creation in its shaping of matter. There floated before my soul a *Philosophy of Freedom*, an outlook on life that sees the world of the senses athirst for the spirit and striving toward it in beauty, a spiritual beholding of the living world of truth.[3]

The same motif, with its stress on the threefold nature of the human being, crops up again a few pages further on:

My *Philosophy of Freedom* is based on experiencing what it means for human consciousness to come to terms with itself. Freedom is *put to practice* in willing, *experienced* in feeling, and *known* in thinking. But the living element in thinking must not be lost sight of in achieving this.

While I was working on my *Philosophy of Freedom* I was constantly concerned to keep inner experience fully present and awake in the thoughts I was setting down. That gives them the mystical quality of inner vision, though that vision retains the character of outer sense perception of the world as well. When one attains to such inner experiencing, one no longer feels any difference between knowledge of nature and spiritual knowledge. One comes to realize that the latter is simply a further metamorphosis of the former.

The fact that I had this impression was the reason why, later on, I gave my *Philosophy of Freedom* the sub-title "Findings of psychic observation, made in accordance with natural scientific methodology." For when scientific method is faithfully adhered to in spiritual investigation, it provides a sound basis for insight in that realm also.[4]

One of the mottos appearing on the dedication page of this volume is taken from Lecture 2 in the series called *Die Geschichte und Bedingungen der anthroposophischen Bewegung im Verhältnis zur Anthroposophischen Gesellschaft*.[5] It tells us something of the purpose intended to be served by *The Philosophy of Freedom*:

Anyone interested in looking for them will find the basic principles of anthroposophy already enunciated in *The Philosophy of Freedom*. Today I only want to emphasize the fact that *The Philosophy of Freedom* constantly points with inner necessity to a spiritual realm, the realm from which we derive our moral principles, for example. This means that in the sense of *The Philosophy of Freedom* we cannot rest content with the physical world, but must continue on into a spiritual world firmly founded in its own reality. That spiritual realm takes on further, concrete reality for us from the fact that man belongs in his innermost being, of which he can become aware, not to the world of the senses but to the spiritual world. These two points: 1) that there is a spiritual realm, and 2) that man belongs to it with his innermost ego-being, are the basic ones made by *The Philosophy of Freedom*.

In this connection it is especially interesting to come upon references to *The Philosophy of Freedom* in a question and answer period that followed a lecture called "Ernahrungsfragen im Lichte der Geisteswissenschaft." [6]

The first question has to do with the fact that many readers of my *Philosophy of Freedom* cannot see any connection between that book and what has just been enunciated here from a spiritual-scientific standpoint seemingly at odds with philosophy by its very nature. The book is out of print at the moment, but will soon appear again in a new edition intended to be an exact duplicate of the first one. This *Philosophy of Freedom* offers what the philosophic approach can contribute on these subjects. A person approaching them on any other basis will always tend to find himself on shaky ground. This book is a philosophically oriented, thinking approach that takes as its starting point the questions, "What is truth?" and "What is the relationship of truth to spiritual science?" I am simply pointing here to what the book has to say about the relationship of thinking to the sphere wherein thoughts originate. Indeed, if it were ever necessary to show that spiritual science does have a philosophical basis, we would have to turn to *The Philosophy of Freedom*. But nobody who realizes that a tree one is painting would look different if painted from another angle will find any contradiction between the two approaches.

In the first lecture of the series "Der Mensch als Gedankenwesen",[7] the fact that *The Philosophy of Freedom* was (and of course still is) specifically aimed at clarifying man's relationship to the spiritual world is again underlined:

Our modern world is still far from being in a position to study man's interwovenness with the cosmos, his at oneness with it. I made a special point of calling attention to this in my *Philosophy of Freedom*, where you will come across key passages intended to show that underneath his ordinary level of consciousness man is related to the entire cosmos, that he is an integral part of the whole cosmos, that his individual humanness, which makes its appearance clothed in ordinary consciousness, blossoms forth as it were from the commonality of the cosmos. Few readers have understood these particular passages in my *Philosophy of Freedom*.

This section must not be brought to a close without including

15

lines taken from the treasure-trove of wisdom embodied by Steiner in verse form, lines in this case related to *The Philosophy of Freedom*:

> When, in the bright circles of the spirit,
> The soul calls forth
> Pure energy of thinking,
> It lays hold on knowledge of what freedom is.
>
> When, entering fully into life,
> Free, conscious man
> Shapes reality from willing,
> Then freedom is made living fact. [8]

CHAPTER III

New Thinking

The artistic element referred to at the beginning of the preceding section is by no means just a matter of composition, of form in movement, of movement in form. Instead, it always bears the hallmark of creativity, shows itself impulsed by creative energy, expresses itself throughout as creative deed. We find all this holding true of *The Philosophy of Freedom*. In its pages the creative energy of the human spirit is trained on thinking itself, with the result that thinking is completely rejuvenated. It is not saying too much to call this a re-creation, a rebirth of human thinking. The form this takes is, of course, conditioned by the necessity of coming to terms with nineteenth century epistemology, but within those limits a new thought current is channeled into humankind. Steiner characterized this creative act in a talk to the workmen at the Goetheanum.* He always spoke before this forum with a directness and simplicity otherwise encountered to some extent only in lectures that he gave in England. Why this was the case in his talks to an audience of workmen can be gathered from the following passages: [1]

> From what I have told you, you will see that although we have a mind or spirit, we need an instrument to work with, and that is the brain. In this physical world we have got to have brains. Materialism has no reason to pride itself on recognizing the necessity for brains; of course we need them. But to assert this is not to state what the spirit is. It shows us besides that the real spirit of a person is able to

---

*Steiner's social impulse led him to give talks during working hours to workmen at the Goetheanum. He did not choose the topics. The talks took the form of genuine conversational exchanges growing out of questions put to him, which he then answered. These conversatins were published as the so-called *Arbeitervorträge* referred to above and in later pages.

withdraw completely, as happens in cases of mental illness. It is important to know this, for it is the only thing that makes us realize that modern human beings simply cannot think. They really can't. I'll show you why it is that they are unable to think.

You will say, "But people all go to elementary schools, and at school they learn to think marvellously nowadays." That may seem absolutely true. Nevertheless, people of the present-day cannot think at all. It just looks as though they can. Now, there are teachers in our elementary schools, aren't there, and they too had to learn something. They supposedly learned to think, among other things. Those who taught them were what Stuttgarters call *"Grosskopfete,"* "big heads," in other words, terrifically wise people, seen from where we stand today. They all went through college. But before that they attended high school, and there they learned Latin. You may do a little investigating and find yourself justified in saying, "But my teacher didn't know Latin." He did study, though, with someone who knew it. What you learned was therefore also affected by the Latin language.... You will have noticed that prescriptions you get are given you in Latin. That is a leftover from times when everything was written in Latin. Lecturing was always done in that language. Study in any field meant immersion in it, and in the Middle Ages every subject was presented exclusively in Latin. You may say, "Surely not in elementary schools!" But we have had elementary schools only since the nineteenth century. They came into being only gradually as the common tongue began to include scientific terms. So that all our thinking has been affected by Latin. All of you think as the Latin language has taught people to think. You may perhaps cite the fact that Americans aren't taught Latin at such an early age. But today's Americans came originally from Europe. Everything has come to be affected by the Latin language.

Now this Latin language has a marked peculiarity. The development it was subjected to in ancient Rome was such that the language itself thinks. It is interesting to see how Latin is presented in high schools. Latin is taken up first, and then thinking, accurate thinking, is taught at hand of Latin sentences. The result is that the whole thinking process comes to depend on the activity not of a person but of the Latin language.

Now please understand what a tremendously important fact this is! Nowadays, people who are supposed to have gone through courses of study are not doing the thinking themselves; the Latin language is thinking in them even though they may never have studied it.

Nowadays, strange as it may sound, we come across independent thinking only in people who have had almost no education.

My point in telling this is not to suggest that we return to an unlettered state; that is not the solution. I'm never for going backwards under any circumstances. But we do have to understand the facts that concern us. This is the reason why it is so important to be able to turn on occasion to simple, uneducated people for information they may still possess in some area.

A person who cannot do his own thinking will never be able to gain access to the spiritual world. Here you have the explanation of why present-day erudition is up in arms against all knowledge of spiritual things; people have been reduced by their Latinized education to an inability to think. So the first thing one must learn to do is to think on one's own. Nowadays people are quite justified in saying that the brain thinks. Why is that the case? Because Latinized sentences enter the brain, and the brain of modern man thinks automatically. We have a collection of automata of the Latin language running about, quite unable to do any thinking of their own.

Something strange happened recently. I mentioned it the last time we met, but it won't have struck you because it is not an easy thing to observe. Something very special has happened in recent times. As you know, we have etheric as well as physical bodies (and other members too, but we don't need to discuss those now). The brain belongs, of course, to the physical body, but the etheric body works in it too. We can think for ourselves only with our etheric bodies; this cannot be done with the physical body. But when it is a case of the brain being used like a thinking machine, as it is with Latin, then one can think with the physical instrument. One can't think spiritually, though, so long as one is thinking with the brain alone. For that, one has to start thinking with the ether body—something the mentally ill often make no use of at all for long periods. It has to be activated by inner effort.

That is indeed what matters most: that we learn to do our own independent thinking! There is no way of getting into the spiritual world without developing that capacity. The first step in that direction is, of course, to begin realizing that we were not taught, when young, to do our own thinking. We were only taught to think as people have been thinking for century after century as a result of using Latin. If we truly realize this, then we also know that the very first requirement for entering the spiritual world is to learn to think entirely on our own.

But now for what I was talking about when I said that something remarkable happened recently. The people whose thinking was most one-sidedly a product of the Latin language were our learned men, and it was learned men who fathered physics, among other things. They thought out physics, thought it out with physical brains as Latin dictates. When we were young, when I was the age of young E. here, for example, the only physics we had was something thought out with people's Latinized brains.... But an awful lot has happened since then. The telephone appeared on the scene when I was a small boy, and all the other great inventions that we now take so for granted followed in its wake. They are all developments of recent times, and they attracted into the scientific field more and more recruits who had not had a Latinized education. It is really a strange business. If you look at scientific developments of the past few decades you will find more and more *technicians* entering the field of science. They had little exposure to the Latin influence and this kept their thinking from becoming automatic. Their non-automatic thinking began to make itself felt in every wider circles. That is why physicists nowadays have thoughts that fall apart so easily. They are very interesting, these thoughts. There is a Professor Türler in Berne, for example, who two years ago commented on the new orientation of physics, saying that all its concepts had changed in recent years. The only reason this has not been noticed is that people who attend popular lectures are still having the outlook of twenty years ago passed on to them! The lecturers can't tell you what is being thought today because they themselves can't think. Taking concepts of thirty years ago and treating them as valid is just like taking hold of pieces of ice that melt in one's hands. The ideas melt away; they just aren't there any longer when one starts subjecting them to exact thinking. We must realize that this is the situation. A person who studied physics thirty years ago and takes a look at what has currently become of it is likely to want to tear his hair out, for he has to see that the concepts he acquired are no longer adequate. What is the reason for this state of things? The reason is that in recent years evolution has brought mankind to the point where the etheric body should become the thinker in us, and people don't want that; they want to go on thinking with the physical body. But in the physical body these concepts simply crumble away, and people refuse to learn to think with their etheric bodies. They don't want to learn to do their own thinking.

That made it necessary for me, back in 1893, to write this book, *The Philosophy of Freedom*. The important thing about the book is not so much what it says (although its message was also something I wanted to get across to the world); the most important thing about *The Philosophy of Freedom* is the fact that in its pages completely independent thinking appears for the first time. A person incapable of thinking freely cannot understand it. He must accustom himself, page by page and right from the outset, to call upon his etheric body if he is to entertain thoughts such as this book presents. It thus serves an educational purpose, and that is how it should be looked at. (Cf. Chapter 10)

Back in the nineties when the book was published, people hadn't the least idea what to do with it. It was as though Europeans had been given a book in Chinese and couldn't understand a thing it said. It was written in German, of course, but in thoughts to which people were entirely unaccustomed, since every trace of Latin influence had been deliberately stripped off. That was the first time anyone had ever devoted himself fully consciously to avoiding Latin influenced thoughts and setting down only those that were fruits of wholly independent thinking. Only the physical brain has an affinity to Latin; man's etheric body hasn't. That is why one has to take pains to express thoughts originating in the etheric body in a way befitting their origin.

This "independent thinking" that is a prerequisite for "seeing the spiritual world" and that was the theme of this lecture to the workmen is thinking that is active through and through. It not only opens the gate to the spiritual world. It also protects mankind from the very present danger of not having thoughts any more, but just words strung together that may pass for trains of thought but are actually the product of a purely automatic process.

People won't have any thoughts at all if they merely let their heads take over. And that is what has happened. We see it in the fact that people don't want to be bothered to think. Interest in thinking is on the wane. What people really want is to have nature dictate their thoughts while all they do is carry out experiments that tell them what to think.... They don't want to have to think for themselves. They have no confidence in their own thinking. For they can't see any reality in what they think out. We can see that thinking— not our thoughts, but thinking as a process—needs energizing. This activation of thinking comes of the spiritual world's playing into it. If you start thinking really actively today, there is no other way of doing it but to let the spiritual world play into you. Otherwise you are not thinking; you are no more thinking than we can say research men are thinking when they follow their favorite procedure of letting experiments and research dictate facts to them, or than social scientists are thinking when, in their disinclination to be active, to come really to grips with social impulses such as only active minds can grasp, they turn to historical research, to inheritances from the past.... A person familiar with these matters knows this. Everywhere we look we find a certain fear of the dawning of a vitally necessary connection with the spiritual world, a fear of really active thinking. That is why anything that calls for active thinking, as my *Philosophy of Freedom* does, meets with so little understanding. The thoughts it contains are different from the thoughts in current fashion, and readers often stop reading the book soon after they begin it for the simple reason that they would like to read it as they do any other. But as you know, other books, books in popular favor, are read sitting leaning back on a chaise lounge, letting thought pictures pass in review before one's mind. Many a person reads everything that way.... Every now and then some little emotion or worry creeps in. But even newspapers, read for the sake of the sensation in them, are read in such a way that the pictures just flash past. But the sort of thing dealt with in *The Philosophy of Freedom* does not allow of that approach. The reader has to keep shaking himself to avoid being put to sleep by the thoughts he encounters. They are not meant for readers who just sit in a chaise lounge. One can read sitting, of course, and even lean back in the chair. But one has to try with all one's human strength to activate one's inner soul-spiritual being, to bring one's whole thinking into motion, aided by the very stillness of one's body. There is no other way of getting forward with it; any other approach puts one to sleep. Many readers do in fact fall asleep, and they are not the least honest ones. The least honest are those who read *The Philosophy of Freedom* as they would any other book and then flatter themselves that they have really taken in the thoughts it contains. They haven't taken them in; they have taken them like empty shells of words. They've kept on reading strings of words without having anything come of it that might be likened to the striking of steel on flint. That is what must be demanded from now on as regards everything that needs to be brought to bear on human evolution, for that will be the means whereby humanity lifts itself gradually and wholesomely into spiritual world. Active thinking will set man's inner relationshi the spiritual world alight, and this will enable him to climb ev higher and higher.[2]

Activity in thinking leads with inner consequence to "aliveness in thinking," an aliveness that represents a further step. It should be emphasized that this aliveness in thinking is the exact antithesis of "deadness in thinking." The latter comes of thinking about things created in the past, things of the sense world, especially those belonging to the mineral kingdom, while the former serves as a means of entering the world of the etheric.

This aliveness in thinking brings you in the end to the experience you will have if you read *The Philosophy of Freedom* as it should be read. To read it properly, you have to know how it feels to live in thoughts. *The Philosophy of Freedom* is something born entirely of real experience, but it is also wholly the product of genuine thinking. That is why you will find a certain basic feeling running through it. I conceived *The Philosophy of Freedom* in the 'eighties, and wrote it down in the early 'nineties, and I can report that I found no understanding for it at all among those people whose job it really was at the time to give at least some attention to the book's major premise. The reason was namely that people—even so-called thinking people of the present—are really unable to do more than reflect the physical world in their thinking. They then say that thinking might possibly convey something of a supersensible nature, but it would have to do so in exactly the way a chair or a table that is actually outside us is present in thought. This thinking that goes on inside us ought somehow to be experienced as though it were an external supersensible element, just as we experience a chair or a table that is there outside us. That is about the way Eduard von Hartmann conceived the task of thinking.

Then he got a copy of *The Philosophy of Freedom*. There, thinking is experienced in a way that makes it impossible for a person involved in it to have any other impression than that, when he is really living in thought, he is living—no matter how unclearly at the moment—in the cosmos. This relatedness to cosmic mysteries that one has in a really inward experience of thinking is the red thread running through *The Philosophy of Freedom*. That is why the sentence, "In thinking we

23

a corner of the secret of the universe" is to be found

the
to
r

.y be a simple way of putting it. But what it means is that it
,sible, in a true experience of thinking, to go on feeling the
mystery to be inaccessible; one is inside it. One no longer feels
,self outside the divine, but within it. *To lay hold on thinking in*
,neself is to lay hold on the divine there.

This was the point people could not grasp. For if one really grasps
it, if one exerts oneself to achieve the experience of thinking, one is no
longer in the world one inhabited before; one is in the *etheric* world.
One is in a world upon which one knows that the earth's physical
spatial being has no influence—a world ruled instead by the whole
universe. One is in the cosmic realm of the etheric. When one grasps
thinking in the sense of *The Philosophy of Freedom,* one can have no
further doubts about the rule of law in this cosmic realm. So one
comes to have what we may call etheric experiences, and achieving it
gives one the feeling of having taken a uniquely decisive step for one's
whole life.

Let me characterize this step. In an ordinary state of consciousness
one thinks, in a room like this, of tables and chairs and people, too, of
course. One may think of other things as well, but they are all things
external to the thinker. Let's say, then, that there is a variety of
objects surrounding us, and from the very center of our beings we
reach out and embrace them with our thinking. Everybody is
conscious of doing this, of making an effort to embrace the things
around him with his thinking.

But if one reaches the point of having the experience just described,
one does not reach out to the outer world or concentrate one's forces
in one's ego center. Instead something quite different happens. One
has the feeling, the absolutely right feeling experience, that one's
thinking, which is really not located in any one place, projects its
power of grasping inward. One has the sensation of feeling out the
inner man. In ordinary thinking, spiritual feelers reach out into the
world. In the case of the thinking that has an inner experience of
itself, one constantly reaches feelers into oneself. We become objects
to ourselves.

This is an important experience that we can have, this realization
that our thinking is ordinarily used to grasp the world around us, but
that we are now using it to lay hold upon ourselves. The result of this

powerful laying hold upon ourselves is that we break throug boundary of our bodies.[3]

This creative act of thinking carried out in *The Philosophy Freedom* in response to the need of the period and conceived as means of bringing the human soul to "aliveness in thinking," is set in the proper perspective among the great events of man's spiritual history (in this case that of Scholasticism) by the following passages, which give it fresh illumination:

The consequence of thinking this thought is that one undertakes the work of tracing the soul-spiritual element right down into the details of the bodily make up. Philosophy doesn't do this, nor does natural science. It can be done only by a spiritual science that does not shy away from bringing down into our own time the great thoughts conceived in the course of mankind's development— thoughts like those produced by Scholasticism—and applying them to what our time has brought forth in the way of views on nature. There had, of course, to be a coming to terms with Kant to give such an effort scientific standing.

This coming to terms with Kant was attempted in three works: in my booklet *Truth and Science,* which came out many years ago; in my short *Theory of Knowledge Based on the Goethe's World Conception,* which appeared in the 'eighties; and lastly, in my *Philosophy of Freedom.* I would like to review for you, briefly and despite the fact that a short treatment makes things seem harder than they really are, the basic thought that lives in these three books.

They start out with the recognition that truth is certainly not to be found directly in the world we see spread out around us. One sees, in a way, how Nominalism gets its hold on the human soul and how it can subscribe to Kantianism's wrong conclusions, but also that what is dealt with in these books is something that Kant did not see at all: the fact, namely, that a really thorough and objective examination of the world perceived by our senses makes us realize that it is not complete in itself, but instead something on which *we* bestow reality.

What was the real root of Nominalism's difficulty? What accounts for the whole rise of Kantianism? The trouble lay in approaching the phenomenal world and deriving from the inner life of the soul a world of ideas that was used to cover it. People came to hold the view that this world of ideas that they had within them somehow mirrored external phenomena. But the world of ideas is an inner one. What *the*

of

r content as man's world of ideas have to do with
oundings? Kant could find no way of answering this
'Well then, let us clothe the phenomenal world with the
as and *create* reality."

s does not conform with the facts. The truth is that when we
r the phenomenal world objectively, we find it everywhere a
al thing, an incompleteness. I tried to give rigorous proof of this
my book *Truth and Science* and again in my *Philosophy of Freedom*. What we perceive must always appear to us in an incomplete form. Through the very fact of entering the world, of being born into it, we split it apart. Here, let us say, [says Dr. Steiner, drawing on the blackboard] is the world content. When we enter the world, we divide it into percepts, which come to us from outside ourselves, and ideas, which come to us from inside our souls. Our very presence in the world divides it for us into a world of percepts and a world of ideas.

Anyone who accepts this division as absolute and says, "There is the world, and here am I," will never be able to get over into the phenomenal world with his ideas. But the facts are as follows. I look at the phenomenal world and see it everywhere incomplete and lacking something. But I myself, with my whole existence, once came out of the very same universe of which the world of percepts is also part. Now I look inside myself, and what this enables me to see is just what is missing in the phenomenal world. I must put together again with my own effort the wholeness that was split in two by my ego's appearance on the scene. My effort re-establishes reality. The fact of my having been born creates the illusion that something whole and complete in itself has split into two separate parts: a perceptual realm and a realm of ideas. By living and growing up and developing, I reunite these two aspects of reality. I work my way back into reality in my search for understanding. I would never have attained consciousness had I not separated the world of ideas from the external world of percepts by being born into it. But I would never find the bridge to an understanding of that world if I failed to restore to union with it the world of ideas from which I sundered it and without which it would have no reality.

Kant sought reality in the external, phenomenal world alone, and had no inkling of the fact that this second half of reality is only to be found in what we carry *within us* as an inner content. We were the ones responsible for divorcing the inner world of ideas from external

26

reality. Now Nominalism is redeemed, for we no longer try to fit over the perceptual world such mere nomina as time and space and ideas. Instead, our insightful approach restores what we robbed the sense world of when we entered it at birth.

Such is the nature of man's relationship to the spiritual world, looked at purely philosophically. A person who opens himself to the basic thought in my *Philosophy of Freedom*—the thought already expressed in the title of *Truth and Science,* namely, that genuine knowledge unites the two worlds of perception and ideas and regards this uniting as a real rather than as an ideal process—such a person participates in the overcoming of Kantianism through his ability to recognize something in the nature of a cosmic process going on in a re-uniting of the perceptual and ideal worlds. He is also involved in a final, effectual dealing with the problem that we have witnessed growing to such proportions in the West's development, giving rise to Nominalism and, in the thirteenth century, shedding a good deal of light as Scholasticism, but impotent in the last analysis to do anything about the split between the world of ideas and the perceptual world.

This problem of individuality is one to be solved in the realm of ethics. That accounts for my *Philosophy of Freedom* turning into a philosophy of reality. Because knowing is not just a formal act, because *it is itself a process in reality*, ethical or moral action comes to be recognized as the end product of a real process taking place in the individual whose moral fantasy has provided him with an intuition. That is what constitutes what I describe in my *Philosophy of Freedom* as *ethical individualism*, which, though the book does not put it that way, actually builds on the foundation of the Christ impulse in man. It builds on the foundation of man's attainment of freedom as he transforms ordinary thinking into what *The Philosophy of Freedom* calls *pure thinking*, a thinking that lifts itself into the spiritual world and brings to birth from union with it impulses to moral action. It does this by spiritualizing the love impulse otherwise bound up with man's physical body. In that moral ideals are drawn from the spiritual world by moral fantasy, they lead to acts as vital as their origin, becoming the energy of spiritual love.[4]

This may suffice to show the nature of the creative act performed by Rudolf Steiner as an artist in the realm of thought. He makes *The Philosophy of Freedom* the birth record of that self-active thinking in which neither the Latin language nor the brain have any share.

27

CHAPTER IV

The Sphere of Freedom

All too often we find people searching for freedom in the realm of man's will, or even in his actions. If they do not find it there, they tend to deny that such a thing exists. If they do believe that they have found it there, they run the risk of confusing it with arbitrary choice. Goethe, in his day, tried to overcome this misconception saying, "Action is easy, thinking difficult. To act on one's thoughts costs painful effort." He thus paints action and thinking as opposites, leaving will as the wellspring of action entirely out of the picture.

The single most vital and important thing about Steiner's "science of freedom" is that it sharply delineates the sphere freedom occupies. It is to be found in the realm of thinking. "Freedom lives in human thinking. The will itself is not directly free; what is free is the thought that energizes will. That is why I had to lay such stress on freedom as an attribute of thought when I discussed the moral nature of the will in my *Philosophy of Freedom*."[1]

The same statement is made in *Die Geistigen Hintergrunde der Sozialen Frage*: You know from my 'Philosophy of Freedom' that to lay hold on moral intuitions puts us in possession of the loftiest moral ideas we human beings need, and that the moral ideas we thus attain to become the foundation of our human freedom.[2]

The mineral kingdom plays an important role in the attainment of this freedom in our thinking:

> ...Only in the mineral kingdom does man possess freedom. That is the sphere where he is free. As he becomes conscious of this fact he also learns to put the problem of freedom in the proper light. If you read my *Philosophy of Freedom*, you will see what importance I lay on not looking for freedom in man's will. The will lies deep, very deep, in

28

our unconsciousness, and it makes no sense to look for freedom there. One can speak of freedom in our thinking only. I made a careful distinction between the two in *The Philosophy of Freedom*. Man is free when free thoughts activate his will. But as a thinker he is indeed a denizen of the realm of minerals.[3]

That is the realm in which human beings develop the thought forms and concepts that enable them to grasp the lifeless world of a past becoming. To the degree that materialism serves this end, it is a method of inquiry to be recognized and acknowledged without reservations. But it is quite a different matter when materialism becomes dissatisfied with its role as an investigative method and claims validity as a way of looking at every aspect of reality.

This thought is carried further in Lecture 3 of the series *Irdische und kosmische Gesetzmässigkeiten*:[4]

> Man's freedom rests on the fact that our thinking is not real unless it becomes pure thinking. A reflection in a mirror cannot make anything happen. When you look at something that is just a mirror picture and react to it, it has not really exercised any compulsion on you. If your thinking contained reality, you could not be free. The fact that your thoughts are only pictures makes your life between birth and death a schooling in freedom. For thinking exercises no compulsion, and a free life must be one in which no First Causes operate.
>
> The life of fantasy, however, is not fully free. But that is to say that it contains reality, that as a life of ideas it is real. To the degree that the life in us is free, it remains unconnected with reality in its thinking aspect. But we do lay hold on reality when we attain to pure thinking, and as a result develop the will to do free deeds. Where we endow pictures with reality drawn from our own substance, freedom of action is possible.
>
> I wanted to demonstrate this fact purely philosophically in my *Philosophy of Freedom* so that it could serve as a foundation for what I would be saying later on.

In Lecture 4 of *Geschichtliche Notwendigkeit und Freiheit*, he puts the matter as follows:

> When a person acts under the influence of pictures reflected in a mirror—in other words, under the influence of his ideas— he is acting

29

out of Maya, out of a reflected world; and since such action has to come from *him*, he is acting freely. When he acts under the influence of passions, or even of feelings, he is unfree. When he acts in response to mental images, to mere reflections, his acts are free. That is why, in *The Philosophy of Freedom*, I explained that a person who acts out of pure ideas, pure thought, is acting freely. For pure ideas cannot of themselves make anything happen; the active agent must be looked for elsewhere.[5]

Lecture 5 of the same series carries this motif further:

Now the question arises as to how we are going to bring the quarter of our soul life that is the sphere of reality to a true experience of freedom. We will have to relate it to something independent of the other three quarters.

I tried to give a philosophical answer to this question in my *Philosophy of Freedom*. I tried to show there that man can only realize his impulse to freedom when he subjects his actions wholly to the influence of pure thinking, when he reaches the point of being able to act on thought impulses rather than on stimuli originating in the world outside him. For nothing that has its origin in the external world permits of our realizing freedom. We can realize it only when we develop impulses to action in our thinking, uninfluenced by the world outside us.... Instead of letting stimuli to will and action rise up out of our physical, astral and etheric bodies, we can shut them out and accept only such impulses as come to us from the spiritual world in the form of imaginations based on underlying inspirations, underlying intuitions. But this need not necessarily be a conscious clairvoyant experience in the sense of saying, "Now I am training my will, based on inspirations and intuitions, on this particular goal." But the fruit of having done so comes in the form of a concept, of pure thinking, that resembles an imaginatively conceived idea. Because that is so, because the concept upon which free action is based must appear to ordinary consciousness like an imaginatively conceived idea, I called the capacity that underlies free action "moral fantasy" in my book *The Philosophy of Freedom*.[6]

The question as to where the sphere of freedom lies becomes especially weighty when we consider human karma, which projects itself out of the past into present necessity. Is that necessity compatible with freedom? This problem is touched upon in Lecture 3 of the series, *Karmic Relationships*.

When we mull over this question, we see that it is indeed a rather weighty one. For all spiritual investigation shows that later incarnations are conditioned by preceding ones. Yet we do most definitely have a sense of possessing freedom. If you read my *Philosophy of Freedom* you will see that we cannot understand man unless we recognize that his whole soul life tends in the direction of freedom, is trained upon and oriented toward it. We need, though, to achieve a right understanding of what freedom is. You will find in this same *Philosophy of Freedom* an idea of freedom that it is extremely important to conceive correctly. The point is that freedom first develops in our thinking, that it springs from thought. Human beings simply possess an immediate consciousness of being free in thinking. [7]

This comment is the more significant for what it does to counteract our human tendency to gaze fascinated at the fact of karmic necessity and become fatalists. There is great danger of that happening. The only way of avoiding it is to see and feel that karmic necessity plays the same rôle in relation to freedom that the solid earth plays in relation to our bodies and the brain to our thinking. All three provide the steady ground for us to move on. The man in whom thinking has rediscovered its origin in the spirit and draws on that source not only frees himself from nature's rule but from karma's as well. The spiritual resource he has found in himself provides him with the possibility of creating something new and fresh and full of promise for the future, something seedlike compared with the necessity issuing from the past.

31

CHAPTER V

New Willing

Now that it has become apparent that the sphere of freedom is not to be sought in the will and still less in action, questions about a new kind of willing can be put in proper perspective and given their due weight. When motive as idea and stimulus as idea coincide, a sphere has been reached in which a person can be guided wholly by his own will's promptings. He has a clear perception both of what is driving him—if the term can still be used in such a context—and of the goal toward which he aims. His ego surveys every element in the picture. Not one of them works the least compulsion on him. His ego itself is having to bestir itself and act. It supplies its own motivation. Thus there is born in him a new, purified will of which he himself is the progenitor. When he applies it, he makes use of the moral fantasy to be described in quotations that follow.

When young people came crowding around Rudolf Steiner seeking his guidance, he replied with the "Youth Course" lectures. As can be seen from the title assigned to the recent publication of this series, he discussed a variety of social problems. [1] The young people's attention was called to one basic problem in a way nothing short of radical:

> Now that the intuitions of the past have been lost to us, we stare into emptiness. What can be done about it? Why, look for the all in the nothing! Strive to find in it something that is not given us without effort on our part, something we have to work to get, and that task was too much for the passive forces that were all we had left. We had to turn to the strongest forces of knowledge at the disposal of present-day man, forces of knowledge inherent in pure thinking. When one engages in pure thinking, that thinking immediately affects one's will. It costs no great effort of will to observe and then think about one's observations, nor does making experiments and

mulling over one's findings call upon the will. But it takes energy to engage in the elemental, original activity of pure thinking. Will's lightning must strike straight into the thinking process, and that lightning must issue from the completely unique individual. The time had come to find the courage to summon up the pure thought that becomes pure will. This will then grows into a new capacity, the capacity to call forth out of one's own individuality moral impulses that are the fruit of effort, that are not simply given us as they were before. From this time on we had to rely on intuitions obtained by individual effort. Our time has no other term but fantasy for what someone thus produces out of his own being. In this age, then, which has made it a practice to discourage inner effort, moral impulses had henceforth to be born of moral fantasy. In other words, people had to be shown how to get beyond merely poetical, artistic fantasy to creative moral fantasy.

That is how the new kind of willing was described to the young people of that time.

The same problem was dealt with from a similar angle in Lecture 8 of the series *Geschichtliche Notwendigkeit und Freiheit*:

Something that has no possibility of being intellectual is the *human will* as I tried to characterize it in its relationship to the impulse of love in my book, *The Philosophy of Freedom*. Human will comes to expression in the subconscious reality of drives or hungers that take the form of a variety of egotistical urges, of social or political ambitions. Everything in this category remains unconscious or subconscious. But when the will is raised to a really conscious level, when what the will impulses otherwise sleep through, or at best just dream through, is lifted into the sphere of consciousness, there is no further possibility of conceiving it materialistically. In our time will is not understood at all, as is apparent to anyone of genuine spiritual insight into a certain symptom of the period. The symptom I refer to is the fact that those who consider themselves the brightest spirits of the age can even raise the question in the way they actually do as to whether there is any such thing as freedom.

The fact that this question is raised is of one piece with other questioning on the subject of man, as, for instance, how he should view himself and what his true being really is.

Man now had to be guided to a rediscovery of his true being. I made an attempt to do this in my *Philosophy of Freedom*. Such was the historical setting of the problem that confronted me as I felt prompted to write *The Philosophy of Freedom*. This "most highly developed animal" in which man is caught cannot be free, nor yet that thought-up human being that is just an idea, with its trappings of "in-itselfness," "out-of-itselfness," "for-itselfness," for that is just a construct of logical necessity. Neither one is free. The only free man is the real human being holding the balance between external material fact and ideas that pierce through to the reality of the spirit. That is why the attempt is made in *The Philosophy of Freedom* to show that moral life is based on the inner experience of morality, called by me moral fantasy, rather than on abstract principles, that it is based on the capacity of the individual as such to draw on intuition.... Detouring thus through moral philosophy, one finds that one has reached the realm of the spirit, and that would perhaps be a way for present-day humanity to achieve understanding of the spiritual world, to realize something that is really not so hard to grasp, namely, that unless morality is conceived to belong to a supersensible, spiritual realm, it has absolutely nothing to stand on.[2]

In the lecture, *Die Harmonisierung von Wissenschaft, Kunst und Religion durch die Anthroposophie,* the problem indicated in the title is brought up in connection with Goethe and Schiller:[3]

Goethe and Schiller are the prime inciters to a really deep and thorough concern with this matter. But in a time so far removed from theirs we must be able to take a free stand in relation to what dawned on them as a significant problem of the human race. As a result of studying these two men deeply and really devotedly when I was getting ready to write my *Philosophy of Freedom*, I came to see the human problem as the problem of freedom. I could simply not be convinced that man is a truly free spirit only when he is occupied with art. Schiller's point, that in gaining insight into the world by acts of knowledge one has to let reason rule and is hence under mental compulsion, is certainly valid. But that is not what we are concerned with here. If one obeys the rule of reason and devotes oneself in this sense to scientific observation, one is living in an experience of *ideas* about nature, about natural laws and the world in general. This means living in images. One feels that one cannot get to the bottom of anything in nature unless one lets free, inner human *activity* hold sway, and that even if natural necessity compels us, it cannot compel us to be *active*; action has to be freely undertaken. One senses the pictorial quality of world and nature, and thus experiences the freedom inherent in one's humanness most poignantly in acts of knowledge. That is what I wanted to demonstrate in my *Philosophy of Freedom*. When one rises to the height of conceiving true impulses to moral action and these impulses become pure thinking, a person thus motivated lives again in pictures. We sense the picture element in our knowing, and if we bring morality to bear on this picture element we feel ourselves in the sphere of freedom.

Here again, then, we find a reference to the picture element in thinking, which, as was shown above, is what human freedom is founded on. This free thinking in turn gives man access to the spiritual world by providing him with intuitions, moral intuitions in particular. These intuitions exercise no compulsion on him, for they come into being as his own creations. Man as ego derives them from the spiritual world. One need only imagine drawing on an actual source like a well or spring, which in this case is the world of the spirit. It is not the spiritual world working from its side on the human being; he has to lift himself up to and draw upon it for his moral ideas, as a person draws water from an everspringing fountain.

The following comments, made by Rudolf Steiner in Leipzig in 1922 on the theme *Agnostizismus in der Wissenschaft und Anthroposophie*[4] speak to the same point:

What foundation can we lay for moral theory, and for spiritual science and sociology as well, in a time when we quite properly recognize phenomenalism to be the suitable approach to outer nature? That was the great question in my mind as I was writing my *Philosophy of Freedom*. I took my stand wholly upon natural science, on a phenomenalistic approach to what can be learned about the outer world of the senses in acts of knowledge. But if one is completely honest in drawing the ultimate consequences of this approach, one has to say that laying an objective foundation for morality calls for a different kind of cognition than that leading to phenomenalism and thus to agnosticism. I refer to a way of knowing that does not use thinking to dream up hypothetical worlds behind the phenomena presented by the senses, but instead makes itself capable of directly perceiving spiritual reality, abandoning the old way of making room for a spiritual element in a mathematically conceived universe.

It is just agnosticism, indeed, that requires us on the one hand to recognize it as wholly legitimate where it applies, but on the other hand to rouse our spirits to the activity needed to grasp a spiritual world, wherein, unless we are content to remain subjective, objective spiritual observation is able to discern the principles of morality.

There was, of course, a certain justification for calling my *Philosophy of Freedom* a work on ethical individualism, but that is just one aspect of it. Of course we have to come to ethical individualism, because the moral principles we behold have to be beheld individually and in freedom.

But just as mathematical problems are worked out in an active inner process as a matter of pure knowledge, yet remain susceptible of objective proof, so may the content of moral impulses be grasped in purely spiritual vision, not just as a matter of belief. That is why one has to say, as I did in my *Philosophy of Freedom*, that a science of morals must be built on moral intuition. I said at the time that the only modern way to achieve a truly moral outlook is to see that we derive moral principles from the spiritual world of our beholding exactly as we isolate single phenomena from the totality of nature—moral principles which, though they are only spiritually perceived, nevertheless constitute objectively grasped reality that exists quite independently of us.

So I spoke first, then, of moral intuition. But this is to indicate a certain direction for the cognitive process. Just because the cognitive process should stay genuinely scientific, it is steered in the direction of rousing the soul to activity and bringing this activation to the point where a beholding of the spiritual world becomes possible.

The difficulties encountered in this striving are described in the second lecture of the series, *Anthroposophie, ihre Erkenntniswurzeln und Lebensfrüchte*:[5]

It is extraordinarily difficult to arrive by this path, purely philosophically, at an understanding of the activity of thinking, and I can fully see how such spirits as Richard Wahle, who recognized the fact that perception offers us nothing but a chaos of impressions, and those other thinkers who really did see only what Johannes Volkelt rightly calls an agglomeration of bits and pieces of external perception that thinking has to bring into some kind of order—I can, I say, understand how these thinkers, entering as they do wholly into

36

the nature of perception, do not reach the point of being able to enter into the nature of the thinking process too. They cannot make the effort necessary to recognizing that when we live in the activity of thinking, we are wholly involved in that activity and can connect it completely with our consciousness. I can well imagine how hard it is for thinkers like these to understand someone saying to them, as a result of fully experiencing this activity of thinking, "In thinking, we actually participate in the world process" —for that is what I stated in my *Philosophy of Freedom*.

The fact that this is the case, that we do actually participate in the world process when we think, could be demonstrated only at hand of the thinking that underlies action and comes into play when we reflect the moral world in the shape given our deeds by our pure thinking. For we are forced at such times to call pure thinking into play, to develop thought in its pure essence, and then, by our own act, to create the percept that belongs to it. The facts themselves compel us to separate perception and thought, to re-connect them afterwards in deeds, in moral action. I showed in my *Philosophy of Freedom* how it is just in pursuit of the ethical, the social life, that the true nature of thought activity dawns on one.

The seventh lecture in the same series describes the concreteness that must be pictured as belonging to this new, thought-saturated will, and what creative energy inheres in it:

The matters presented by anthroposophical spiritual science are not the product of some vague mysticism; every step that led to a particular insight can be accurately traced. The path it follows, far from being external, is an inward one from start to finish, but it is of such a nature that it leads to an experiencing of true, objective, *supersensible* reality. But in lifting oneself to truly *intuitive cognition* in this way, one arrives for the first time at a true understanding of what this thinking of ours really is—this conceptual life that we apply in everyday living and with which we permeate what we perceive. One arrives at the full, complete reality of that of which one can form some first empirical idea in the way I tried to indicate in my *Philosophy of Freedom*. I tried to show the nature of pure thinking, the thinking that can go on in us before we have related this particular aspect of thought to any external percept and thereby rendered reality complete. I pointed out that this pure thinking can be perceived as an inner content of the soul, but that its real nature can be known only when the soul reaches the stage of true intuition as it travels the path of higher knowledge. Then a person really comes to understand this thinking of his. He lives into this thinking for the first time with the help of intuition. For intuition is simply a living into the supersensible with one's own being, an immersion of the self in the supersensible.

So one comes to learn something that, as I have just suggested, is in the nature of a destined experience of knowledge. One experiences something tremendous as one lives intuitively into the nature of the cognitive process. Then one comes to know how man's physicality is organized and what purposes it serves. But intuition also enables one to see that it serves only as a base upon which thinking can develop, that the material processes themselves have to be broken down for genuine thinking to take place. To the degree that material processes are broken down, thinking or conceiving can occupy the place cleared by this material destruction....

Intuition also enables us to understand how the substantial matter in man's organism is expedited from the metabolism to the place where it is to be broken down by the will, which now takes its motivation from pure thinking. Thinking as such destroys; the will builds up. This up-building process does indeed remain latent in the human organism all through life, but it is there. Thus, when in our moral motivation we rise to truly free moral intuitions, we live the kind of human life that brings the will into play to expedite transformed matter from our organisms to the place where matter has been broken down. Such a person becomes inwardly creative, inwardly a builder. Put another way, we see an empty place in the cosmos of the human organism filled out with *new construction*, quite material new construction, which means nothing less than that a person who travels the path of anthroposophical cognition with consequence arrives at a point where purely moral ideals become a world building element within him, right down into material substance.

This is to discover the moral world as a creative force, to see how something comes into being to whose reality human morality can bear witness because it is its own offspring, its own creation.

Here the presentation of the new willing reaches one high point. The moral order is the product of human creativity, brought to birth in freedom out of the spiritual world. This creative moral force is matter-forming.

*　　*　　*

Now let us turn our attention to a quite different aspect of the problem. In June 1919, Steiner gave a lecture in Heidenheim entitled *Some Characteristics of Today*[6] in which he said:

At that time I tried to point out something in a certain area that represents a drastic need of the present. Of course, due to the crudity, the philistinism of modern science, the monstrosity that passes for orthodox science at the universities nowadays, it was not understood. I called one chapter of my *Philosophy of Freedom*, which came out in 1894, "moral fantasy." From the spiritual scientific viewpoint it could also be entitled "imaginative moral impulses." I wanted to show that the realm otherwise dealt with only by the artist in imagination must now become the serious concern of the human race, for the reason that it represents the stage mankind must reach to lay hold upon the supersensible that the brain is incapable of grasping. At the start of the 'nineties I wanted to show that at least in regard to understanding morality a serious attempt was being made to grasp the supersensible. These things should be sensed nowadays. We should have some feeling for the fact that the thoughts, the inner soul impulses that were being lived out right up to the time of the catastrophic World War and the period of social upheaval were no longer useful, and that new impulses were required.

Here we are shown the new willing depicted in the context of its social mission.

We close this section with an excerpt from a lecture entitled *The Knowledge of the Spiritual Being of the Universe*:[7]

Already in the early 1890's I showed in my *Philosophy of Freedom* how a person wholly dedicated to the modern natural scientific viewpoint can find a relationship to the moral world. One actually discovers that this natural science can go even further than it has gone in the past, applying all its thinking exclusively to the penetration and ordering of external phenomena and so arriving at laws that can be summed up in thought form. One comes to realize that this approach to nature cannot of itself gain access to the supersensible. Everything it achieves in the way of inner soul experience is simply a picturing of the outer sense world, and such it necessarily remains.

But it is just when we bring thinking to the perfection to which the natural scientific age has brought it, just when our scientific attitude is not amateurish, but instead fully in accord with the rigorous, exact methods of modern research, that we gradually achieve an inner experience of thinking that is nevertheless free of any physical or bodily element.

That is generally a bit difficult for the humanity of recent times to grasp. But it is just the person who has gone deeply into modern science who makes the eventual discovery that there is an element in his thought life that the body has no share in mediating. In my *Philosophy of Freedom*, which I wrote in the early 'nineties, I called this element "pure thought life" and its functioning "pure thinking." I attempted to show that it is just when a person applies scientifically schooled thinking, stripped of all personal instincts, whims and fantasy, to understanding a natural world quite outside the bounds of morality and to which he can form no sort of religious relationship, when he develops real power in his thinking about nature, that individual, personal moral impulses make their way from deep inside him into this scientifically developed pure thinking of his. We need only look without preconceptions into nature, not stopping short there but instead relating back to ourselves, to find that the more truly scientifically we think, the more truly we experience this scientific thinking, the more powerfully does the element I called moral intuition penetrate our pure thought process. Then our relationship to the world is such that we can say, "Yes, nature as we now see it has been stripped of divinity; it has become an amoral realm. But in our role as thinkers about nature, human beings feel just this purest of scientific thinking that we engage in permeated in the end by moral intuitions from within ourselves, exactly as we perceive blood flowing into our physical heads to provide us with a physical instrument for thinking."

CHAPTER VI

New Thinking, New Willing
The Thinking — Will

On New Year's Eve 1922, the Goetheanum building went up in flames, taking with it the work of many years. Despite all the pain and shock that this event occasioned, however, the work went on without interruption. The situation called for a new effort, for it was not just the building that lay in ruins: the Society itself was in equally bad case. Both edifices had to be rebuilt and Rudolf Steiner set to work on both tasks with the fiery will over which he disposed.

The lectures he gave at the larger centers were all on the subject of reshaping the Society. In Stuttgart he spoke "words of pain and a searching of conscience," the emphasis of which was more on past events. Another lecture followed at the end of January. Then came one on February 6th in Stuttgart, called "New Thinking, New Willing," from which we quote at length. This lecture outlines the tasks to which the Anthroposophical Society needed henceforth to address itself, showing their relationship to *The Philosophy of Freedom*.

There are two aspects here that seem especially important. Steiner often called attention to the fact that this book illuminates the nature of man's relationship to the cosmos. He even said on occasion that it does so "in a particularly appropriate manner." But his comments on this point remain quite general. The lecture does, however, indicate the book's cosmic placement with its concrete references to Saturn and Moon. And this placement must appear the more significant since mankind has become involved in attempts, carried out wholly externally, with technological aids such as rockets, etc., to launch itself into cosmic space. For the past seventy years it has been possible to do

41

that on a purely inner path, as Steiner's comment on *The Philosophy of Freedom* shows.

There is obviously no question here of an "either-or" choice between efforts of the soul and spirit on the one hand and perfected technological achievements on the other. A balance must be created between the two possibilities. Neither the technological nor the soul-spiritual path can exist all by itself and become the solely determining one. Both belong together, as do outside and inside, hull and kernel, body and soul.

The last part of the quoted passages may seem almost more important for immediate application. It amounts to an appeal to read *The Philosophy of Freedom*, and to read it in the way it should be read. The point is made that proper study of this book gives the reader an inner attitude that, for all its humility, enables him to stand entirely on his own feet in relating to anthroposophy. It teaches him to present it on his own authority rather than on that of someone else, who in any event never even wanted to be considered an authority in the wrong sense of the word:*

> I would like to refer back to my book, *The Philosophy of Freedom*, which was published three decades ago, and I would like to call attention to the fact that I described in its pages a special kind of thinking very different from that generally recognized as thinking nowadays. When thinking is mentioned—and this holds especially true in the case of those whose opinions carry greatest weight—the concept of it is one that pictures the thinking human spirit as rather passive. This human spirit devotes itself to outer observation, studying phenomena or experimenting, and then using thought to

---

*A confirmation from the author's personal experience: Wolfgang Wachsmuth, manager of the publishing house, Der Kommende Tag, and the editor of this book were at a conference with Rudolf Steiner. In the course of the conversation, Steiner made the statement, "Nobody in the Anthroposophical Society possesses as little authority as I do," whereupon he was confronted by two incredulous, puzzled faces. "You don't believe it? I'll give you an example. When the idea of building a theatre for the mystery plays was conceived, I was asked to design it. When I had done so, the question if its probable cost was raised. I answered, '5-6 million marks,' for I know how these things go. Thereupon they asked an architect, who estimated 5-6 hundred thousand marks. They believed him instead of me. You see how much authority I possess in the Anthroposophical Society." Then he added with a twinkle, "But the building did turn out to cost what I estimated."

relate these observations. Thus it comes to set up laws of nature, concerning the validity and metaphysical or merely physical significance of which disputes may arise. But it makes a difference whether a person just entertains these thoughts that have come to him from observing nature or proceeds instead to try to reach some clarity as to his own human relationship to these thoughts that he has formed at hand of nature—which, indeed, he has only recently acquired the ability to form about it. For if we go back to earlier times, say to the thirteenth or twelfth or eleventh centuries, we find that man's thoughts about nature were the product of a different attitude of soul. People of today conceive of thinking as just a passive noting of phenomena and of the consistency—or lack of consistency—with which they occur. One simply allows thoughts to emerge from the phenomena and passively occupy one's soul. In contrast to this, my *Philosophy of Freedom* stresses the active element in thinking, emphasizing how the will enters into it and how one can become aware of one's own inner activity in the exercise of what I have called pure thinking. In this connection I showed that all truly moral impulses have their origin in this pure thinking. I tried to point out how the will strikes into the otherwise passive realm of thought, stirring it awake and making the thinker inwardly active.

Now what kind of reader approach did *The Philosophy of Freedom* count on? It had to assume a special way of reading. It expected the reader, as he read, to undergo the sort of inner experience that, in an external sense, is really just like waking up out of sleep in the morning. The feeling one should have about it is such as to make one say, "My relationship to the world in passive thoughts was, on a higher level, that of a person who lies asleep. Now I am waking up." It is like knowing, at the moment of awakening, that one has been lying passively in bed, letting nature have her way with one's body. But then one begins to be inwardly active. One relates one's senses actively to what is going on in the color permeated, sounding world about one. One links one's own bodily activity to one's intentions. The reader of *The Philosophy of Freedom* should experience something very like this waking moment of transition from passivity to activity, though of course on a higher level. He should be able to say, "Yes, I have certainly thought thoughts before. But my thinking took the form of just letting thoughts flow and carry me along. Now, little by little, I am beginning to be inwardly active in them. I am reminded of waking up in the morning and relating my sense-activity to sounds

43

and colors, and my bodily movement to my will." Experiencing this awakening as I have described it in my book, *Vom Menschenratsel,* [1] where I comment on Johann Gottlieb Fichte, is to develop a soul attitude completely different from that prevalent today. But the attitude of soul thus arrived at leads not merely to knowledge that must be accepted on someone else's authority but to asking oneself what the thoughts were that one used to have and what this activity is that one now launches to strike into one's formerly passive thinking. What, one asks, is this element that has the same rousing effect on one's erstwhile thinking that one's life of soul and spirit has on one's body on awakening? (I am referring here just to the external fact of awaking). One begins to experience thinking in a way one could not have done without coming to know it as a living, active function.

So long as one is only considering passive thoughts, thinking remains just a development going on in the body while the physical senses are occupying themselves with external objects. But when a person suffuses this passive thinking with inner activity, he lights upon another similar comparison for the thinking he formerly engaged in, and can begin to see what its passivity resembled. He comes to the realization that this passive thinking of his was exactly the same thing in the soul realm that a corpse represents in the physical. When one looks at a corpse here in the physical world, one has to recognize that it was not created as the thing one sees, that none of nature's ordinary laws can be made to account for the present material composition of this body. Such a configuration of material elements could be brought about only as the result of a living human being having dwelt in what is now a corpse. It has become mere remains, abandoned by a formerly indwelling person; it can be accounted for only by assuming the prior existence of a living human being.

An observer confronting his own passive thinking resembles someone who has never seen anything but corpses, who has never beheld a living person. Such a man would have to look upon all corpses as miraculous creations, since nothing in nature could possibly have produced them. When one suffuses one's thinking with active soul life, one realizes for the first time that thought is just a leftover and recognizes it as the remains of something that has died. Ordinary thinking is dead, a mere corpse of the soul, and one has to become aware of it as such through suffusing it with one's own soul life and getting to know this corpse of abstract thinking in its new

44

aliveness. To understand ordinary thinking, one has to see that it is dead, a psychic corpse whose erstwhile life is to be sought in the soul's pre-earthly existence. During that phase of experience, the soul lived in a bodiless state in the life element of its thinking, and the thinking left it in its earthly life must be regarded as the soul corpse of the living soul of pre-earthly existence.

This becomes the illuminating inner experience that one can have on projecting will into one's thinking. One has to look at thinking this way when, in accordance with mankind's present stage of evolution, one searches for the source of ethical and moral impulses in pure thinking. Then one has the experience of being lifted by pure thinking itself out of one's body and into a realm not of the earth. Then one realizes that what one possesses in this living thinking has no connection whatsoever with the physical world, but is nonetheless real. It has to do with a world that physical eyes cannot see, a world one inhabited before one descended into a body: the spiritual world. One also realizes that even the laws governing our planetary system are of a kind unrelated to the world we enter with enlivened thinking. I am deliberately putting it in an old-fashioned way and saying that one would have to go to the ends of the planetary system to reach the world where what one grasps in living thinking has its true significance. One would have to go beyond Saturn to find the world where living thoughts apply, but where we also discover the cosmic source of creativity on earth.

This is the first step we take to go out again into the universe in an age that otherwise regards itself as living on a mere speck of dust in the cosmos. It is the first advance toward a possibility of seeing what is really out there—seeing it with living thinking. One transcends the bounds of the planetary system.

If you consider the human will further as I have done in my *Philosophy of Freedom*, you find that just as one is carried beyond Saturn into the universe when the will strikes into erstwhile passive thinking, so one can advance on the opposite side by entering deeply into the will to the extent of becoming utterly quiescent, by becoming a pole of stillness in the motion one otherwise engenders in the world of will. Our bodies are in motion when we engage in willing. Even when that will is nothing more than a wish, bodily substance comes into movement. Willing is motion for ordinary consciousness. When a person wills, he becomes part of the world's movement.

Now if one does the exercises described in my book, *Knowledge of*

45

the Higher Worlds and its Attainment, and thereby succeeds in opposing one's own deliberate inner quiet to this motion in which one is caught up in every act of willing, if—to put it in a picture that can be applied to all will activity—one succeeds in keeping the soul still while the body moves through space, succeeds in being active in the world while the soul remains quiet, carries on activity and at the same time quietly observes it, then thinking suffuses the will just as the will previously suffused thinking.

When this happens, one comes out on the opposite side of the world. One gets to know the will as something that can also free itself from the physical body, that can even transport one out of the realm subject to ordinary earth laws. This brings one knowledge of an especially significant fact that throws light on man's connection with the universe. One learns to say, "You harbor in your will sphere a great variety of drives, instincts and passions. But none of them belongs to the world about which you learn in your experiments, restricted as they are to the earthly sense world. Nor are they to be found in corpses. They belong to a different world that merely extends into this one, a world that keeps its activity quite separate from everything that has to do with the sense world."

I am only giving you a sketch of these matters today because I want to characterize the third phase of anthroposophy. One comes to enter the universe from its opposite side, the side endowed with its external character by the physical moon. The moon repels rather than absorbs sunlight; it leaves sunlight just as it was by reflecting it back from its surface, and it rays back other cosmic forces in a similar way. It excludes them for it belongs to a different world than the one that gives us the capacity to see. Light enables us to see. But the moon rays back the light, refusing to absorb it. Thinking that lays hold on itself in inner activity carries us on the one side as far as Saturn; laying hold on our wills leads us on the other side into the moon's activity. We learn to relate man to the cosmos. We are led out of and beyond a mere grain of dust earth. Learning elevates itself again to a concern with the cosmos, and we rediscover in the universe elements that live in us too as soul-spiritual beings. When, on the one hand, we have achieved a soul condition in which our thinking is rendered active by its permeation with will and, on the other hand, achieve the suffusion of our will with thinking, then we reach the boundaries of the planetary system, going out into the Saturn realm on the one side while we go out into the universe on the other side and enter the moon sphere. When our consciousness feels as much at home in the universe as it does on earth, and then experiences what goes on in the universe as familiarly as our ordinary consciousness experiences things of earth, when we live thus consciously in the unverse and achieve self-awareness there, we begin to remember earlier earth lives. Our successive incarnations become a fact experienced in the cosmic memory to which we have now gained access.

It need not surprise us that we cannot remember earlier lives on earth while we are incarnated. For what we experience in the intervals between them is not earthly experience, and the effect of one life on the next takes place only as a result of man's lifting himself out of the realm of earth. How could a person recall his earlier incarnations unless he first raised his consciousness to a heavenly level?

I wanted just to sketch these things today, for they have often been discussed by me here before. What I had in mind was to indicate the regions in which, in recent years, anthroposophy has been carrying on its research. Those interested in weighing what has been going on surely recall how consistently my lectures have concerned themselves in recent years with just these realms. Their purpose was gradually to clarify the process whereby one develops from an ordinary consciousness to a higher one. Though I have always said that ordinary thinking can, if it is unprejudiced, grasp the findings of anthroposophical research, I have also emphasized that everybody can attain today to a state of consciousness whereby he is able to develop a new kind of thinking and willing, which give him entry to the world whereof anthroposophy speaks. The essential thing would be to change the habit of reading books like my *Philosophy of Freedom* with the mental attitude one has toward other philosophical treatises. The way it should be read is with attention to the fact that it brings one to a wholly different way of thinking and willing and looking at things. If this were done, one would realize that such an approach lifts one's consciousness out of the earth into another world, and that one derives from it the kind of inner assurance that makes it possible to speak with conviction about the results of spiritual research. Those who read *The Philosophy of Freedom* as it should be read speak with inner conviction and assurance about the findings of researchers who have gone beyond the stage one has oneself reached as a beginner. But the right way of reading *The Philosophy of Freedom* makes everyone who adopts it the kind of beginner I am describing. Beginners like these can report the more detailed findings

47

of advanced research in exactly the same way in which a person at home in chemistry would talk of research in that field. Although he may not actually have seen it done, it is familiar to him from what he has learned and heard and knows as part of reality. The vital thing in discussing anthroposophy is always to develop a certain soul attitude, not just to project a picture of the world different from the generally accepted one.

The trouble is that *The Philosophy of Freedom* has not been read in the different way I have been describing. That is the point, and a point that must be sharply stressed if the development of the Anthroposophical Society is not to fall far behind that of anthroposophy itself. If it does fall behind, anthroposophy's promulgation through the Society will result in its being completely misunderstood, and its only fruit will be endless conflict! [2]

The following quotation is taken from a lecture entitled "Der Nachtmensch und der Tagesmensch," given in Dornach on February 3, 1923, [3] three days before the lecture quoted immediately above. It is on the same theme dealt with at the end of the Stuttgart lecture with its statement that the thinking will enables a person to guarantee the truth of anthroposophy with his whole self, for in his thinking will he experiences that truth at its first level:

The situation that accounted for that earlier state of soul was that man had not yet developed the pure thinking of more recent times. The latter, of which mention is made fully consciously for the first time in my *Philosophy of Freedom*, is something people have little feeling for thus far. This pure thinking is a development we owe to natural science.

Let us consider astronomy, an aspect of science that provides a particularly characteristic example of what I am about to describe. Copernicus was responsible for turning astronomy into a kind of cosmic mechanics, making it the description of the running of a cosmic machine. Prior to this, there was still some awareness that spiritual beings were embodied in the stars. The Scholasticism of the Middle Ages still speaks of the spiritual nature of the stars and of the intelligences that live and are embodied in them. It is only recently that people have thought of everything up there as material and void of thought, as something that only man ever thinks about. In earlier times, people connected pictures with the appearance of a star or constellation; they saw something living in it, something carrying on an existence of its own. It was not pure thinking that connected man with his environment; it was a quality of soul life. But human beings have developed pure thinking in relation to it...[4]

For centuries now, beginning with the 1400's, man has been educated to this passivity of concepts. Nowadays he even regards it as a form of sinning to be inwardly active and to think for himself. Indeed , one cannot think for oneself on the subject of nature. To do that would be to sully nature with all kinds of fantasies. But the source from which thinking springs is in oneself. One can think for oneself, and even impregnate the thoughts one already has with inner reality, since they are just thoughts. And when does this happen? It happens when a person summons up enough strength to project his night-self into his day-time life, when he is not just giving himself up to passing thoughts but projecting himself into them with all the independence he has attained while sleeping. He can do this only with pure thinking.

That was actually the basic theme of my *Philosophy of Freedom*. I pointed out there that modern man can really project his ego being into the thinking to which he has presently attained. He can now project into the activity of pure thinking the ego being over which, as modern man, he freely disposes while he sleeps. I could not state this at that time, but it is a fact. A person becomes truly conscious of his ego being in pure thinking when he enters into thoughts in such a way as to live actively in them.

Let us picture anthroposophy being presented along the lines of a modern scientific presentation. The listeners would take it in with the passive thinking to which modern human beings are accustomed. Anyone with a healthy mind can surely understand it. But the way people live in such thoughts is passive, just like the way they live in thoughts about external nature. Then they come along and say, "I got these ideas from anthroposophical research. I can't vouch for them myself; I simply adopted them." A lot of people say, "I got this from spiritual science." How often do we not hear that "science tells us this or that," and "spiritual science teaches us this or that"? What does it mean when someone says he has learned something from spiritual science? It means that he is showing us that he is mired in passive thinking and wants to take up spiritual science with an equally passive kind of thinking. For the moment he makes up his mind to

49

reproduce in himself the thoughts offered by anthroposophical research he will be able to vouch for their truth, having then experienced that truth at its first level. [5]

In his lecture, "Freedom and Love", Steiner goes so far as to identify thinking with willing: "....When thinking has become pure thought, we can just as well say that it is pure willing."[6] He makes a distinction, however, between the ways the two faculties interpenetrate each other. Freedom is the irradiation of thought-life by the will, love the suffusion of the will with thinking (cf. *The Philosophy of Freedom*, Chapter 3).

Now, we have the possibility of becoming wholly free—free in our inner life, that is—if we succeed in shutting out any thought content based on externalities while at the same time raising to high intensity the will element that rays through our thoughts when we form judgments or draw conclusions. This means turning our thinking into what I termed pure thinking in my *Philosophy of Freedom*; we think, but will alone lives in the thinking process. This is an aspect on which I laid particular stress in the 1918 edition of the book. What lives in us then lives in the thought sphere. But when it has become pure thinking, it can just as correctly be termed pure willing. We rise to the level where we transform thinking into will when we achieve inner freedom; we ripen our thinking to the point where it is wholly irradiated by our will, no longer letting outer stimuli affect it, but living wholly in the will. But it is just through strengthening the will element in our thinking that we equip ourselves for what in *The Philosophy of Freedom* I called moral fantasy, a faculty that reaches up to the sphere of moral intuitions, which then suffuse and irradiate our thought-become-will or our will-become-thought. Thus we lift ourselves above the level of natural necessity, imbue ourselves with something that is peculiarly our own, and ready ourselves to exercise moral intuition. In the last analysis, moral intuitions account for everything that comes from the spiritual world and fulfills human nature. Freedom comes alive in us as a result of making will ever more powerful in our thinking process.

Now let us consider man from the opposite pole, the pole of willing. When does will show up unmistakably in our actions? When we sneeze we can also be said to be doing something, but we can scarcely ascribe it to a particular impulse of our will. When we speak, however, we are doing something where will is to some extent involved. But just think what a mixture of the voluntary and the involuntary, the willed and the unwilled, is present in speaking! You have to *learn* to speak, yet do so in a way that does not require forming every single word with an act of will; an instinctive element has to enter into speaking. This is true in ordinary life at least, and is apt to be characteristic of people who are not particularly keen spiritual strivers. But the more we disengage ourselves from the organic element in us and go on to activity rid of involvement in it, the more do we permeate action with thinking. Sneezing is wholly ascribable to organic causes, and speaking too, to a great extent. Walking is much less so, and so are the things we do with our hands.... Unless we are sleepwalkers and act in that state, our actions are always accompanied by thoughts. We imbue our actions with our thinking, and the more developed our action is, the more thought permeated is it.

You see, we become ever more inward as we project our individual energy into our thinking and send our will raying through and through it. We project will into thinking, and as we go on refining our behavior we arrive at the point of embodying thoughts in it. We send our thoughts raying into the actions being born of our will. From the outside in, we live a life of thought, and irradiating it with our will we arrive at freedom. Conversely, from within outward, our actions flow forth from our wills, and we imbue them with thoughts.

But what is the refining element at work on our actions? What accounts for our rise to increasingly perfect levels of behavior? We perfect it increasingly by nurturing that capacity in us that can only be described as *devotion to the world around us.* The greater our devotion to it, the more this surrounding world incites us to action. But it is just by finding the way to devote ourselves to the outer world that we attain the ability to permeate our deeds with thoughts. For what is devotion to the world around us? This devotion that fills us and permeates our deeds with thoughts is simply love.

Just as we attain to freedom by raying will into our thought life, so do we attain to love by permeating our will life with our thinking.

Only weak minds could picture the world made up of unchanging, everlasting atoms. If we think in accordance with reality, we picture matter continuously being done away with to the zero point, and then being built up again out of nothingness. It is only because new matter is constantly being created to replace matter that has disappeared that people talk of the indestructibility of matter. They are victims of the same misconception they would be subject to if they mistook for the originals copies of documents that had been taken into a building, copied, and the originals burned there. Since what is brought back out again looks like what went in, people mistake it for the same thing, whereas what actually happened was that the originals were destroyed and duplicates made of them. That is what happens in the world's developmental process, and it is vital that human insight progress to the point of understanding this. For where matter is done away with in man and disappears, to be replaced by newly created matter, there we find the possibility of freedom, and there too the possibility of love. Freedom and love belong together, as I indicated in my *Philosophy of Freedom.* [7]

Already in 1895 Steiner set down in the pages of a guest book a saying that expresses the motif of *The Philosophy of Freedom*, one that points in the same direction:

"The lover's eyes are blind to the beloved's weaknesses,"
Runs the old saying.
It never seemed to me the right statement of it,
For I would say that only loving eyes see truly,
Since only they perceive the loved one's virtues. [8]

The lecture entitled "Der übersinnliche Mensch und die Fragen der Willensfreiheit und Unsterblichkeit, nach Ergebnissen der Geisteswissenschaft," [9] calls attention to passages in *The Philosophy of Freedom* that have a significant bearing on this topic:

Twenty-five years ago, it seemed to me particularly important to enter a protest in a philosophical work against a widespread misconception, a misconception that can be summed up in the phrase, "Love makes us blind." I showed that, on the contrary, love makes us seeing. It guides us into an area we cannot enter if we remain egotistically isolated in our own selfhood, and it does this the moment we are able to sacrifice our selves sufficiently to live with our feelings in another's being, to live within it for the very reason that we hold its independence sacred and have no desire to impinge upon it with our love. We cannot call a love perfect that wants to meddle with the nature of the loved person and make changes in it. We love truly when we love a person for his own sake, to the point where the one who loves forgets himself. When we feel love for someone wholly independent of ourselves, someone whom we love especially well just because we are conscious of his separateness, and have no slightest desire to influence him in any way tinged with our egotism, when we love him purely for his own sake rather than for ours, then this feeling to which we can rise is truly the ideal of the love that, I am convinced, makes us seeing, not blind. This love can be developed for an *action*, for what we find needs doing when we give ourselves up to pure contemplation of some action. Among the many and varied actions born of our desires and instincts there can be others that at least move in the direction of the kind of impulse that carries out an action purely out of love for it. This is the other point I brought out at that time in my *Philosophy of Freedom*, with the statement that a person who examines the idea of freedom soon comes to realize that only such actions as are born in this sense out of the impulse of love can possibly be free. For the moment this can be taken only as an observation, but it helps to form at least some idea of the quality inherent in free action. One comes to realize that one is not justified in calling any other kind of action free. The only question is whether it is possible for actions of this kind to be included in human life, whether actions born of love can become a reality in human living.

Even if we recognize that such a thing as action born of love is possible to human life, we can probably still not call man free in the entirety of his being, but must rather say that he comes closer and closer to freedom the more he transforms his behavior in the direction of making his deeds acts performed out of love.

But one does not arrive at an understanding of these two matters I have been characterizing if one approaches them in the spirit of a purely external, conceptual study. They can only be grasped with the help of spiritual-scientific methods that I must now proceed to describe to you. My various books have gone thoroughly into the measures—exercises, if you will—that the soul has to undertake in order to perceive the spiritual world as clearly as physical eyes perceive the sense world. Today, however, I want to call attention to a point especially suited to throwing light on the two matters I have been characterizing....

Twenty-five years ago, I applied the term "intuitive thinking" to what I am now describing as an attribute of pure thinking born of intuition and making its appearance in moral rather than in logical concepts when a person acts in accordance with moral ideas. "Moral fantasy" was the term given to what such a person perceives living imaginatively within him. When one becomes aware that an unconscious inspiration lives at one pole of his being and an unconscious imagination at the other, he becomes aware of his immortal part. Though in ordinary life this awareness remains at an unconscious or subconscious level, it is nevertheless present. It is present in unconscious inspirations, as also in moral ideas, regardless of whether they are right or wrong; it is present on occasions when we are not taken up with ourselves, but develop—in warmth of love for an action such as I described—an energy that carries us beyond the confines of self-interest.

Here something remarkable reveals itself in human nature. When something that is otherwise present only at an unconscious level, namely, this unconscious imagination that is a personal possession and that, as I described, can only be made effective by love, works in concert with intuitive or inspired thinking as this shines in from its own sphere to illumine ideas... when this thinking, that is born not of man's mortal part but of what is immortal in him, works in concert with the imagination that ordinarily remains unconscious but takes on an instinctual character in us when we conceive love for an action...when, as I say, this instinctive love, which is an instinctual expression of the imagination described, acts on a person in such a way as to move him to make use through inspiration of what shines into him from the time before his birth, then an immortal element works on the immortal element in man. An idea, born of the immortal world that we experience before our birth, works in concert with the immortal element that manifests itself on an unconscious level in imagination and returns again to the spiritual world through the gates of death.

Thus man is capable of actions in which his immortal part, otherwise revealed only after death, becomes an effective force during his earthly life and works in concert with free ideas issuing, through inspiration, from the immortal realm in the form of impulses that enter our human personalities before birth. This is then *free* deed.

This freedom of action is a human potentiality, and man is aware of possessing it. One learns to understand what freedom is only when one knows that unconscious imagination, which builds toward our life after death, works in concert with unconscious inspiration, the latter a force emanating from our life before birth and playing into our souls. When a person instinctively performs actions prompted by the

54

immortal being in him, he is doing free deeds, and the fact that he is aware of acting freely is a reflection, the *Fata Morgana* cast by something—his immortal part—that lies deep in the supersensible component of human personality.

Man's relationship to freedom...is not such as to justify saying either that he is free or unfree. In his ordinary actions he is both; he is on the way to freedom. But he does not become aware of his freedom until he becomes aware of man's immortal being.

Today, in closing, I want to sum up in two sentences what I have been developing for you here in a spiritual-scientific survey of freedom of action and the soul's immortality. What I have been trying to show is that freedom cannot be understood without grasping immortality, nor can immortality be understood without regarding freedom as the consequence of its reality. The immortal human being is a free human being, and the will that springs from what is immortal in him is free will.... Our ordinary actions tend in that direction. Mortal man is en route to freedom. As mortal man goes on making the immortal man in him ever more conscious, he becomes aware of his freedom. *Man is born to freedom, but he must educate himself to realize it.*

The Philosophy of Freedom is not only the primal source of a new thinking, but of a new willing, issuing from that new thought. This gives rise to a willing that is love as well. Ethical individualism thus becomes the foundation of true social action.

CHAPTER VII

Transition to the Social Problem

A lecture, again given in Stuttgart, concerns itself wholly with *The Philosophy of Freedom*. Steiner had been invited to deliver a public lecture at the Siegle House on the contemporary situation, and he refers to the book right at the beginning of the section to be quoted. The theme he chose for his talk was "Fragen der Seele und Fragen des Lebens."[1] It begins with a rehearsal of the aims that *The Philosophy of Freedom* was intended to serve. He goes on to speak, as he had before on the subject of love, of social trust as the second force that must come to permeate our living. The following chapter makes it obvious that he touches here on the book's innermost nerve. We quote at length from this wide ranging lecture:

> At the start of my lecture tonight I am going to permit myself to describe how the question, "How can present-day humanity create a single and harmonious whole of the path the soul travels and of life as we live it?" hovered before me when the 'eighties were drawing to a close, when—on the basis of the viewpoint at which I had arrived over a long period of years—I was working out my *Philosophy of Freedom*, which appeared in 1894. In the form in which I was able to present it at that time, the book was intended to serve as an answer to humanity's question as to its destiny, expressed at the beginning of our considerations tonight.
>
> It is not my intention to talk today about the content of this *Philosophy of Freedom*. But I do want, by way of introduction, to touch briefly on the book's underlying aims.
>
> A basic objective was to give an answer to the question as to how a person set down in the present and confronted by its tremendous challenges can make his peace with the time's most significant feeling and longing: the feeling and longing for *freedom*. It is just in considering the nature of freedom that we can surely see how essential

56

it was to break with the way people had been questioning the validity of the idea of freedom, the impulse to freedom. People were asking, "Is man by nature a free being, or is he unfree?" The whole development of man in the age we live in seems to render this question no longer timely. After all humanity has gone through in the past three or four centuries, we can really only ask today whether man is in a position to build a social order that enables him, as he grows from childhood to maturity, to find in himself something that he is justified in calling freedom. The question I put was not whether man is born a free being, but whether it is possible for him to find something deep down in himself that he can fetch up from an unconscious or subconscious realm into the clear light of full consciousness, and whether, doing so, he can develop himself into a free being.

This enquiry led me to see that there are only two factors on which this most vital element in mankind's recent development can be based, that is, on what I called at the time *intuitive thinking* and *social trust*. Because what I meant by these two terms was nothing in the least abstract or theoretical, but on the contrary something absolutely real and vital, it took a long, long time for what was meant in this book to come to be understood...

So I tried, in my *Philosophy of Freedom*, to show how man must come again to the point of doing more than just filling his consciousness with a content gathered from nature such as modern science offers him in its concepts and ideas. I showed that wellsprings of an inner life can be opened up in man's own being. When he grasps this source of inner soul life, when he grasps the soul content that is not a product of sense observation but has its origin in the soul itself, then he educates himself through understanding this soul content to free decisions, to free willing, to free deeds.

I tried to make clear in my *Philosophy of Freedom*, that one remains dependent if one responds to natural impulses only, that one can become free only by reaching the point of responding to the promptings of intuitive thinking as it develops in one's soul. This indication of the quality of soul that one has to achieve through self-development before one can partake of genuine freedom led to my necessarily making the attempt to carry to a further point what had been hinted at in *The Philosophy of Freedom*. I have been trying to do this for the past several decades in the form of what I have called anthroposophically oriented spiritual science.

For after calling attention to the fact that human beings have to

57

derive the impulse to freedom, to intuitive thinking, out of the depths of their own souls, one must also show what happens when a person draws upon this inner source of his soul life. The anthroposophically oriented expositions of the years that followed are actually all just statements of matters to which I called attention at the time of writing my *Philosophy of Freedom*.

I pointed out that there are paths the soul can follow to the development of a thinking that is not summed up in an intellectual piecing together of a picture of the world, but instead goes on to lift itself in inner vision to an experiencing of the spirit. I felt impelled to describe what it is one sees on looking into the spiritual world.

In the present age, however, one must emphasize that the nebulous mystical approach many people have in mind when they refer to the inner wellsprings of the soul, the vague floating and vaporizing that abandons itself to an inner dream state, is not what was meant.

But this led to a twofold outcome. For one thing, those who had no desire to undertake something looked upon nowadays as uncomfortably demanding, that is, the pursuit of clear thinking, were little attracted to anything that went in the direction taken by my *Philosophy of Freedom*. The other was that too many floaters and dreamers, seeking experience on all sorts of nebulous, unclear paths, attached themselves to what anthroposophically oriented spiritual science was trying to achieve in clarity. This following attracted the attention of a lot of ill-disposed persons who now attack what people with whom I have no connection whatsoever have been saying. But in these attacks they attribute to me everything that these floaters and vaporizers, these vague mystics have produced as their own twisted version of something just particularly intended to meet the urgent needs of modern culture. For one of the things most centrally needed is *clarity on the path of inner striving*, a clarity of inner striving comparable to the clarity of external striving that distinguishes the true scientist but, as I said, a clarity of *inner* striving. That is one thing very much needed: not darkness and dimness, not vague mysticism, but brightest clarity in everything that has to do with thinking.

That is one need. The other is the *social trust* that needs to serve as the basis for what I was talking about in my *Philosophy of Freedom*. We live in an age in which every single human being has to find within his own individual consciousness the direction for his thinking, his feeling and his will to follow. We no longer live in a period in which people can really endure letting themselves be led by authority, or having their whole being organized from outside. As a matter of fact, organizing has only made its appearance as a kind of counter-balance....

If the fountainhead of what in my *Philosophy of Freedom* is called true intuition is opened up in humanity, we will be able to base communal dealing with life's higher concerns on trust, exactly as we have to deal on a basis of trust in our everyday affairs. For if two people are about to pass each other on the street, it wouldn't do at all for a policeman to step up and direct one of them how to manage so as not to bump into the other. The matter of course way in which we handle ordinary life can be extended to life's higher levels if the proper seriousness is there and can be cultivated.

This *Philosophy of Freedom*, however, did discuss two prerequisites of the soul path. One was not to rest satisfied with the kind of thinking that is popular today, popular both in science and in everyday living, but to rise instead to the cultivation in man of something that the new age we live in is demanding, namely, a thinking that flows forth from a primal source of its own in human souls, a thinking full of light and clarity....

The second aspect of the education and development of the human race that we are discussing here leads to man's becoming unified in the experiencing of his will impulses, right down into his very body. The second transformation made possible by spiritual science is the spiritualization of the body by the will, the projecting of the will into every aspect of sense activity and bodily functioning, and into everything of a social nature.

What becomes of one's ideals when the body is thus impregnated with them as a result of practicing a spiritual-scientific thinking method? These ideals are laid hold of by something that our bodies otherwise direct only toward the world of the senses round about us. The capacity for love, love as the senses know it, with which our bodies endow us in a gradual awakening throughout our youth, takes on, in those really dedicated to spiritual science, a character such that all their ideals become something more than mere abstractions, more than mere thoughts; they are loved, loved with all the strength of one's humanness. The spiritual basis of our morality, our ethics, our code of behavior, our religious aspirations, is loved as we love a beloved human being, a flesh and blood person. That is why *The Philosophy of Freedom* had to overcome every trace of the abstract categorical imperative that so disturbed Schiller in his time because it was an element in human life that required submission.

When a love impulse of the kind described becomes a driving force in human society, *trust* is made the basis of its common life. Person relates to person in an entirely individual way, not like one of a herd of animals kept in order by some sort of organization and directed from outside as to what course to follow.

So I can say that at that time—the beginning of the 'nineties—I very much wanted my *Philosophy of Freedom* to sound a clarion call for the exact opposite of what we see happening today in the frightful, murderous events taking place in Eastern Europe and spreading from there to infect other areas, including a large part of Asia.

Developments of recent times brought about social conditions in which perverse human instinct pursued a direction completely counter to what a grasp of present-day humanity's true and deeper goal required our taking. That is the terrible tragedy of modern times. It makes it absolutely necessary for us, in our efforts in future, to recognize that the social order must be built in a way that is made possible only by free thinking, by trust, by what Goethe had in mind when he was looking for a definition of duty and said, "Duty is loving what one orders oneself to undertake...."

In putting forward *The Philosophy of Freedom* and the anthroposophically oriented spiritual science based upon it, I never hid the fact that I was unconcerned with this or that particular statement, this or that detail. I have always spoken with some irony of the people who are chiefly interested in hearing how many parts man consists of or what is to be discovered in this or that area of the spiritual world. I always spoke ironically of this trend. But what I *was* concerned with was to answer the question: what becomes of the whole human being, of his human bearing in body, soul and spirit, when he takes the trouble not to *think* along the lines dictated to him by the merely natural science of our day, not to *will* as various organizations train him to do, but who instead thinks and wills in the sense of *The Philosophy of Freedom* and an anthroposophically oriented spiritual science. I was always pointing out that the thinking engendered just by taking in this spiritual science becomes lively and mobile, that it makes for a broad interest in present-day concerns and develops a free and open sense for seeing what it is that keeps us from progressing in our human evolution.

There is surely no other passage that brings out so unmistakably what a great and universally human goal *The Philosophy of Freedom* was intended to serve. The book represents no mere side-branch of philosophy. Rather is it the foundation of a new branch of science—the science of freedom—and this not just in the sense of supplying knowledge of what freedom is, but of making this a science of freedom co-equal with the natural and spiritual sciences. Its methods are philosophic, based on psychological observation. Its style is that in which cognitive theory was couched at the time of its appearance.

If this science of freedom does not receive the same intensive cultivation accorded other aspects of science, freedom will be irretrievably lost, both by society as a whole and by the individual. Warnings on the score of certain prevailing world conditions are clear enough, and the book not only shows how materialism can be overcome (cf. the Introduction); it points the way too to an overcoming of materialism's social consequences.

CHAPTER VIII

The Socially Oriented Will

But this is what I want to show you. Nothing can be achieved today with abstract programs and so-called ideals, no matter how impressive they may sound. Nowadays one simply has to find out what people want. But this will never become clear in negotiations with them, for they are anything but ready to reveal what is going on in them in such negotiations. One cannot just negotiate or talk with them; one must learn to think and feel with them. One must also feel a sense of obligation about making use of what karma brings one and carry out its intended purposes. The amount of good that can come of the frightful storms about to break over us will depend entirely on whether people make up their minds to develop an understanding of matters such as, for example, what I inaugurated with my *Philosophy of Freedom*. I'm sure you will agree that everybody does what in him lies, what his karma dictates. I want to single out among the things I myself have undertaken the development of thoughts capable of providing a structuring of social life, thoughts that, a quarter of a century ago, in the early 'nineties, I hoped would find a sounding board, thoughts that I hope again today will find a sounding board after a quarter of a century has passed and a second edition of the book has appeared. I hope they will find a sounding board not in spite of the hard times just beginning, but precisely because of them.

Such was Steiner's description of the social aspect of his task as characterized in the lectures entitled *Entwicklungsgeschichtliche Unterlagen zur Bildung eines sozialen Urteils.* [1]

Even though he agreed in earlier statements to his standpoint being called "ethical individualism," he does express some reservations about so designating it. Ethical individualism? Well, yes, provided that doesn't lead to individuals stressing their separateness, but rather to their developing such a capacity for ideas that each thinker is fully as able to enter into others' thoughts as into his own. To succeed in doing that is to make ethical individualism a socially productive system of ethics, to join people rather than to separate them. For it means that they are inhabiting a common supersensible world. That spells a transition from the consciousness soul to spirit self, as was suggested in the Introduction. In "Grundideen der Goeth-Studien"[2] we find this indicated:

> An action carried out in the spirit of Goethe's system of ethics is ethically free even though it may have a natural cause, for man depends exclusively on his own ideas and answers to no one but himself. In my *Philosophy of Freedom*, I exposed the error in the superficial objection that a moral order in which everyone obeyed only his own dictates would result in general chaos and lack of coordination between one man's actions and the next's. A person raising this objection fails to consider that human beings belong to one and the same order and therefore never produce ideas so essentially different as to make for disharmony.

A whole string of questions of course arises at this point. One such would be, "What gave rise to the ideologies of the West and the East, which not only contradict but combat each other?"

Primitive though the answer may sound, it is nevertheless an accurate statement of the facts: Neither the East nor the West reckons with man as a spiritual being. The West—and this includes Bolshevism—sees in him just a bodily being, a material object, to which it concedes a few soul aspects. The Church sees him as a being of body and soul, which indeed he is, but aside from granting him a few spiritual attributes, limits him to these. The result is that anyone who looks upon individual man as the possessor of a spirit is regarded as a heretic, while anyone mentioning the word soul is a reactionary.

Such are the Church and Bolshevist positions. Both take their stand on the belief that man is not endowed with spirit.

Steiner's socially oriented will, however, goes straight back to man's spiritual origin, as will be evident from the following quote.[3]

> What anthroposophical knowledge enkindles in us with its pursuit of the supersensible is love of man. It teaches us how precious a

63

human being is and imbues us with a feeling for human dignity. Recognition of man's worth, feeling for man's dignity, a love imbued will—these are life's fruits, garnered as one learns to experience the findings of spiritual science. In this process, spiritual science stimulates the will to a capacity for what I have described in my *Philosophy of Freedom* as moral intuition. The tremendous effect on human life is that these moral intuitions become permeated by an element otherwise experienced as human love, that we can become human beings acting freely by virtue of the power of love inherent in us as individuals....

I felt that I had to speak in *The Philosophy of Freedom* of how beautiful human morality appears when it is indistinguishable from freedom and springs from genuine human caring. But anthroposophy is in a position to show how this love of duty goes on growing into love of man and thus becomes the real quickener of social life. We can gain insight into the huge, burning social problem that confronts us today only if we take the trouble to realize the connection between freedom, love, man's being, spiritual and natural necessity.

We encounter a different aspect of the social problem when we concern ourselves with the immediate relationship between person and person. Thus far we have looked at it from the standpoint of an individual's capacity to be as receptive to another's being as to his own. The forces involved are the same as those described in the preceding quotation. But now the focus of interest shifts to the question of how one individual relates to another in their life together. The discussion revolves around the fact of our falling asleep in encounters with our fellowmen, and waking up again when we "come to ourselves." Coming to oneself is antisocial, but it is nevertheless essential to the preservation of the ego. Waking up in encounters with other human beings is what makes social beings of us. This falling asleep and reawakening is closely related to what Rudolf Steiner says about experiencing one's own and someone else's ego: [4]

The perception of the ego is that of an entirely negative reality, and it is extremely important to recognize this fact. We need to see through the nothingness of the shallow ego concept held by many philosophers of recent times. Only when we have seen the facts for what they are will we be able to understand, understand from inside, how person relates to person in life.

I described this relationship in one of the addenda to be found in the new edition of *The Philosophy of Freedom*. Not only do we perceive our own ego, albeit negatively, as I just described; we also perceive the ego of our fellowman. We could not perceive it if the ego were in our own consciousness. If it *were* there, the relationship of one person to another would be a very awkward business, for we would go through the world with our minds and senses always aware of just one thing: ego, ego, ego. We would pass other people with the feeling that they were nothing more than shadows, with a sense of surprise—if we stretched out a hand—that it did not go right through their bodies. We would simply be unable to explain to ourselves why it was that we couldn't put a hand right straight through them. This would have the effect of causing us to experience the ego as substantial rather than merely as the mental picture in our minds and senses of a negative reality. We do not have the ego in our consciousness. We have it only in our willing and in the feeling element that radiates from willing. That is where we really find the ego, not actually in the life of our minds and senses.

When we perceive a fellow human being, it is our willing that really does the perceiving. These days, many who fancy themselves philosophers entertain the following crazy notion. We look at a person standing there before us and see a particular appearance— hair on top, a forehead below it, then a nose, a mouth, etc., etc. We have often seen ourselves in the mirror and realize that we look just like the man standing there before us. *We* have an ego, so we extrapolate and draw the conclusion that this man also has one. This is a crazy notion, absolute nonsense. For the fact is that we perceive the other man's ego in exactly the same way that we perceive our own, albeit as a negative reality. It is just because our ego is not in our consciousness, but outside it, as our willing is, that we are able to enter into his ego nature. If the ego were in our consciousness, we could not project ourselves into another person's ego, and would perceive him only as a shadow among shadows.

How, then, does our perceiving of him actually take place? Well, it is a highly complex process. We stand there confronting him. He claims our attention, so to speak, and puts us to sleep for a tiny moment; he hypnotizes us and puts us briefly to sleep. Our sense of humanhood is as though actually put to sleep for a split second. We resist this and assert ourselves. So it goes, like a pendulum-swing: falling asleep in the encounter with the other person, waking up in ourselves; falling asleep, waking up. This pendulum-like swinging between falling asleep in someone else and waking up in ourselves is the complex process that takes place in us in our encounters with our fellowmen. It is a process that goes on in our willing. We are unaware of it, however, for we do not have the slightest perception of our willing. But this constant vibrating back and forth does indeed take place, as described in my *Philosophy of Freedom*.

Now if one searches the book for the passage Steiner is referring to, one comes upon a few lines on this preeminently vital matter in the first addendum to the new edition of 1918, but they are not easy to find. This is typical of Steiner's teaching method. An all important matter such as this is treated as though it were a mere side issue; a comment leads to a theme's comprehensive development in a whole series of lectures that approaches this fundamental social phenomenon from every imaginable angle.*
(See following page for footnote)

A further aspect of the social problem comes to light in a confrontation with socialism, that is, with the teachings of Karl Marx. Here, as elsewhere, Steiner finds no fault with theories read from the realities of social life. But he brings other realities into the picture to put Marx's misconceptions straight. One reality that Marx left out of his reckoning is the fact of human individuality, and it is not hard to understand Marxists rejecting anthroposophy as "individualistic."

Soon after the close of World War I, Steiner gave a whole series of lectures intended to awaken some understanding of the social problems of the present.[5] In the second lecture he says:

What we see coming is indeed a confrontation between the proletariat that has grown out of the industrialism of the past several centuries and the old class structure of the human race. I expressed my views on the matter to some extent when, referring to my *Philosophy of Freedom*, I stated what I would consider the most essential thing to undertake at that moment, and still so consider. But I would like to make the following comment. The important thing is to see that a movement is developing with a certain elemental necessity. I am referring to the social movement, to the sum total of the social challenges being presented by the proletariat, and we have got to be able to get to the bottom of what is actually in the making here, not merely express this or that opinion on the subject.

Further comments by Steiner illustrate the factual rather than the critical or opinionated approach needing to be taken to the rising tide of socialism. He says:

What must we realize if we are to understand the socialization process? Karl Marx simply had no feeling for man as a nerve-sense being, for the fact that he is an individual, and that as an individual he is more than any society has it in its power to give him. That is what I had to stress in my *Philosophy of Freedom*, which touches the innermost nerve of the social question in its discussion of this theme. This is the point that has to be made in commenting on Karl Marx's theory of socialization, which completely loses sight of the individual, just as one has to point out the function served by the earth and the soil and the mental labor involved in socializing the means of

---

*"What do I actually have before me in the person of a fellow human being? I consider first his most obvious aspect, his bodily appearance, which comes across to me as immediate perception. Then I perceive what he is saying, and so on. And I do not content myself with simply staring at him: my perceptions set my thinking working. As I engage in thinking in the other's presence, I realize that these perceptions are transparent and let me see the soul behind them. As I think about them I have to conclude that they are by no means what they appear to be to my external senses. The appearance to the senses as immediately perceived also conveys a further, indirect perception. It no sooner confronts me than it is extinguished as mere sense appearance. But what emerges from its extinguishing, forces me, as a thinking being, to empty out my own thoughts for the moment and replace them with the other person's, which I then experience in my own thinking process as though they were mine. I have thus actually perceived the other's thinking. For my thinking lays hold on what has been extinguished as an immediate perception appearing to the senses; a process takes place in my full consciousness whereby the other's thinking replaces my own. The extinguishing of the sense appearance actually does away with the separation between the two spheres of consciousness. This is reflected in my consciousness in the fact that, as I live in the content of the other's consciousness, I experience my own as little as I would in dreamless sleep. In that condition my own day waking consciousness is obliterated, and the same situation obtains as I open myself to perception of the content of the other person's consciousness. We fail to realize this only because, for one thing, consciousness is not followed by unconsciousness in the act of perceiving the other person as it does when we are falling asleep; rather does the other's content of consciousness replace our own; and secondly, because the change-over from the one content of consciousness to the other takes place so swiftly as ordinarily to go unnoticed." *The Philosophy of Freedom*, Anthroposophic Press, Spring Valley, New York, 1972, pp. 220-221.

production. For here again it can be demonstrated that the whole social process would have to come to a standstill if the founts of human individuality were to cease flowing and providing it with what it needs. [6]

Other comments in line with the above were woven into these lectures, for example, "Man is actually what he is by virtue of the elemental forces inhering in him as an individual. I tried to demonstrate this as scientific fact in my *Philosophy of Freedom.*"

The anti-individualism to which Marxism tends is described as follows in Lecture 8 of the same series:

Marxism has given the proletariat of today the feeling that the point of view of the single man, the individual, counts for nothing in the real progress of the human race. It regards the single person's convictions as important only in areas where his own private concerns are involved...whereas everything that makes history happens as a result of objective economic developments.... The conflict that my *Philosophy of Freedom* got me into with the modern proletariat came of my insisting that everything be based on the content and the fact of human individuality, the very thing to which modern proletarian concepts granted no importance. All that the proletariat had any feeling for was man the social animal, the social creature. It saw society as the source of all progress, of everything good that has come about in the course of history. [7]

One further, lightly ironic comment from the same lecture, referring to *The Philosophy of Freedom*:

People think that anything done by an agency other than the State cannot possibly benefit the human race. This opinion is a fairly recent development, by the way. For the nineteenth century was fairly well along when an insightful man wrote the impressive treatise called "Ideas conceived in an attempt to set limits to the function of the State." The man who wrote it was Wilhelm von Humboldt, a Prussian minister of state. I was most particularly taken by this treatise because in the nineties, and even on into the twentieth century, my *Philosophy of Freedom* was always listed under the heading of "individualistic anarchy." This was not of my doing; others were responsible for its placement. Wilhelm von Humboldt's "Limits of the state's function" always headed the list. My *Philosophy of Freedom* was usually at the bottom as the chronologically last entrant. So you see that it was possible to be listed among writers on "individualistic anarchy," but at least in the company of a Prussian minister of state.[8]

We close this section with a passage from the series *In geänderter Zeitlage*:[9] "The basic fact here is that every human being is an individual. I tried in my *Philosophy of Freedom* to establish this as a fact in the face of the levelling inherent in Kantianism and Socialism."

CHAPTER IX

Forces at Work in the Contemporary Scene

The importance of the following section and of the quotations that appear in it can be gauged properly only upon studying the lecture given by Steiner on the occasion in 1918 of the publishing of the second edition of *The Philosophy of Freedom*. This lecture was discussed above in another connection and significant excerpts from it are to be found in the Introduction. We need to refer to it again as we go on to consider the forces at work in the contemporary scene. Only a short passage will be quoted here.

> Now that *The Philosophy of Freedom* is being brought out again a quarter of a century after its first appearance, I would like to emphasize that it was born of an intensive experiencing of the nature of the times, of really feeling them out, of an attempt to discern the impulses astir behind them. Now, twenty-five years later, after the catastrophe that has broken over the human race, I see that this book was indeed truly of its time, even if in the strange sense that people of the time have not developed anything of what the book advocates, and often don't even want to hear about it. [1]

If the above may be said to typify Steiner's prevailing mood, the sentences below would seem to follow in direct connection:

> What, indeed, is this Socialism we see developing but the product of something that flourished during the centuries known as the Middle Ages, something that the culture of more recent times has not eradicated from the mind of the masses? Even though the adherents of Socialism seem outwardly to be hostile to the various religious confessions, their thought forms are wholly in line with them. The present-day natural scientist, the layman with his popularization of the modern outlook, the theoretical socialist, all bring the selfsame thought forms to bear on the indestructibility of matter and energy that the man of the Middle Ages applied to his efforts to grasp a supernatural God. The new vision that has to be developed has been

70

set forth for many years now.... What we need to realize is that the threefold social organism, which is the social approach that we are fostering, follows of necessity from recognizing the need for a renewal of thinking, for a rebirth of thinking out of the spiritual world. This reborn thinking is the only thing that can teach us how to build the bridge that recent centuries, right up to the present, have been unable to build. I am speaking of the bridge between the world of natural fact, which people insist on approaching from the angle of natural causation, and the world that has its source in man's inner being, the world of morality, of religious elevation, of a religious conception of the universe. Only if we work up the courage to think energetically along the lines of this approach can we develop any clarity as to what the needs of the present are, both as regards an outlook on life and social orientation.

Such is the permeation with a quality of inwardness, owing to its origin in knowledge, of the existence of a divine-spiritual world, of the spiritual-scientific world view that I have been describing. It recognizes the fact that the divine is just as fully present in man's inner experience of thought about the world and in the individual or communal working of his human will as it is in the natural world outside him.

That is what I wanted to express in my *Philosophy of Freedom* back in the beginning of the 'nineties, and what is again being brought to expression with a new edition of the book. It was written with the purpose of building a true bridge between the contemplation of nature and those impulses indwelling in the human race that must be born of freedom and cannot bring forth a sense-making social structure out of anything but freedom. But there is one prerequisite. That is the cultivation of a rather more inward cast of thinking than the sleeping souls of the present have in common.[2]

Here we have a comprehensive indication of what the times need to make progress possible. A great variety of aspects was brought up for discussion. The following year[3] Steiner again referred to a critical point in time that impelled him to search for solutions to the period's need.

The real effects that agnosticism had had on all human life were most acutely noticeable at the time when I was succeeding in finding a way to get at the roots of what I now call anthroposophy. My first search for them began in the 1880's. Anyone interested in tracing that search will find evidence of it in writings prepared by me as introductions to the scientific works of Goethe, namely, *Goethe's Erkenntnistheorie*, my short book, *Truth and Science* and *The Philosophy of Freedom*, which appeared in the early 1890's.

Quite a different aspect of the time's need is discussed in the lectures *Man in the Light of Occultism, Theosophy and Philosophy*[4]:

The ancient revelations that sprang from earlier forms of occultism have been lost to the human race. Occultism gradually developed new forms that were little understood by the outside world. A new understanding must be created for it in our time, a time in which it must reappear as theosophy.

But there was an interval during which people no longer looked up to the occult truths that had once been proclaimed to them, and they had no understanding for what we are presenting today as theosophy. They clung to the last vestiges of a higher trinity: matter, soul and spirit. Out of this view of things, which had lost its bearings only because it no longer had access to the ancient revelations, there grew something that first appeared on the scene about six centuries before Christ and that has lasted into our own time, namely, philosophy. You will find in every case that philosophy follows as the next in line upon the last outward revelation of the great trinity, which itself remains veiled. Philosophy perceives nothing but the material scene that human consciousness is gnawing away at. It has no understanding for the Inexpressible Word, but does have some feeling for the soul element in the world when that element reveals itself in the human soul as the spoken Word. It cannot penetrate to the Unrevealed Light, but has a sense for it because that light appears in its most external manifestation as the activity of human thinking, the function of the human spirit that was first oriented toward the outer world. Body, soul and spirit, known to the Greeks as threefold man, have played an important role throughout the philosophic era. There came a time during which everything occult or theosophical was hidden from the outer world, and people gave their allegiance to the most external aspect of revelation, to what is known as body, soul and spirit. This era has continued on into our time, but now philosophy has had its day. The philosophers have seen the last of their era. The only role philosophy can play today is the preservation of that human possession, the ego, the consciousness of self, which the clairvoyant has to be able to remember at the first stage of his development. Philosophy will have to realize this. Try to understand my *Philosophy of Freedom* from this angle. It joins forces with just those elements that have to carry philosophy forward into the era to come, a time in which theosophy—a truer reflection of the higher trinity than philosophy—must re-enter human evolution.

The end of philosophy is foreseen here. It is assigned a certain task, that is, the preserving of a consciousness of self. Looking at such a book as *The Riddles of Philosophy* or *Vom Menschenrätsel* from this angle, one finds them both taking the step referred to. Both end in a preview of anthroposophy. Thus *The Philosophy of Freedom* carries out that great mission of the human race: the re-opening of the gates of the supersensible world that Aristotle barred or, perhaps more accurately, locked.

There is a lecture called "Geisteswissenschaft, Gedankenfreiheit und soziale Kräfte," given by Steiner in Stuttgart on December 19, 1919,[5] that goes intensively into what was moving the period. It also goes into what Steiner had to offer compared with Woodrow Wilson and his thought world:

> And there is a close connection between the spiritual science being presented here and that demand of the times, which is more than a century old and which I must describe as a demand for freedom of thought. What it is calling for is social *freedom*.
>
> It is strange how consistently it happens nowadays that when one tries to understand what the turbulent sea of social challenge is bringing to the surface, one is confronted again and again with the necessity of looking into the question of human freedom, of grasping that impulse that shows itself, in one form or another, to be an impulse to freedom. That this is an important point was a fact that impressed itself even upon Woodrow Wilson, the man whom I consider the most unfortunate figure among the so-called prominent men of the time who have made their influence felt on the course of events.
>
> I am going to speak again today about Woodrow Wilson in exactly the same way I always did on neutral soil during the war years when he was so worshipped by everybody.There are numerous places in his writings where he points out that events—and he knows the American situation best—can be turned in a wholesome direction only by

73

meeting the challenge of man's striving for freedom. How does Woodrow Wilson look at human freedom however? We come across an interesting trend in modern thought when we go into this question, for Woodrow Wilson's thinking is indeed representative. You find him expressing the following view in his book on freedom. He says that one gets an idea of freedom by looking at a cog in a machine. If it fits so well that the machine runs smoothly, we say that the cog is "functioning freely." Or, to take the case of a ship, it must be so constructed that its engines accomodate themselves to the motion of the waves, that they adjust to it, that they run freely in harmony with the watery element. He compares the smooth running of a cog in a machine or of a ship on the ocean waves with an ideal exercising of the human will to freedom. He says that a person is free when he functions as freely as a cog in a smoothly functioning machine, when he moves without causing any stoppage, when he fits freely into the external scene with his energies and moves as part of it without feeling any friction. It is a highly interesting thing that this peculiar view of human freedom could spring from the modern scientific attitude and approach, for isn't it the very opposite of freedom to be so geared-in to the way things are that one can function only as they dictate? Aren't there occasions when freedom actually requires us to be able to oppose the prevailing outer circumstances? Must we not rather equate freedom with elements in a ship that enable it to go counter to the waves and bring it to a stop if need be? What is the source of this strange Wilsonian outlook, which, far from holding any promise of wholesome statesmanly insight, could only spawn the fourteen abstract points of Wilson's proclaiming, which were unfortunately the object of some veneration for awhile, even here in this country?

That is why our time fails to see that we must take recourse in human thought as such, in thinking that is grasped in its nature as thought, and which, if we are talking about real freedom, is the only source from which human life can derive truly free impulses. That is what I was trying to show, more than thirty years ago, in my *Philosophy of Freedom*, which has recently reappeared with pertinent additions. Of course, I made the attempt in it to conceive the impulse to freedom a little differently than is currently the fashion. I tried to show how mistaken the way of putting questions about freedom is. People ask, "Is man free or unfree? Is he a free being with the capacity to make his own responsible decisions, or is he bound up in natural or spiritual necessity, as nature's creatures are?"....

Freedom is just as much a child of thinking, of thoughts conceived not under duress from any outer source but in clairvoyant spiritual perception, as it is the child of genuine, devoted love, love for the object of one's action. What German spiritual life was striving for in Schiller when he opposed Kant and had a premonition of such a concept of freedom is what it behooves us to develop further in our day. But then I found that one can speak only of the basis of moral actions, of something that is present in man even though it remains on an unconscious level, something that must be termed intuition. So I spoke in my *Philosophy of Freedom* of *moral intuition*. That was the starting point for everything I tried to accomplish later on in the area of spiritual science. I surely know that this *Philosophy of Freedom*, which was conceived over thirty years ago when I was young, bears all the pockmarks of the children's diseases that afflicted the life of thinking as it developed in the course of the nineteenth century. But I also know that something came of that experiencing of the spirit that lifted this thought life into a realm truly of the spirit. So that I can say that when a person rises to the level of ethical impulses in moral intuition and demonstrates that he is truly free, he is already "clairvoyant" with respect to those intuitions. All ethical motivation belongs to a realm occupying a place far above that of the senses. Genuine ethical commandments are really always products of clairvoyance. Thus a straight path led from *The Philosophy of Freedom* to what I am presenting nowadays as spiritual science. Freedom is attained only as a result of developing oneself. But a person can go on developing himself, so that what already forms the basis of his freeom is carried to a further stage, a stage at which he becomes independent of the sense world and lifts free into the regions of the spirit.

That is the way freedom is related to the development of human thinking. At bottom, freedom always signifies freedom of thought. Looking at representative men like Woodrow Wilson, we have to say that they can invent paradoxical definitions such as Wilson came up with in the case of freedom only because they have never grasped what spiritual realities thoughts are, and that thoughts, to be anything but abstract, must have spiritual roots. This is just the sort of thing that shows us what the intellectual life of the day is lacking, what renders it unfit, in its ignorance of man's spiritual nature, to supply with its mental life a real basis for the freedom of thought so vitally needed, and to fill the chief requirement, that of meeting the challenge of

75

social forces by buiding this life of the mind into a tool that will be equal in future to the three great demands making themselves felt in the present scene.

Now let us come back again to the lecture Steiner gave when the second edition of *The Philosophy of Freedom* appeared, a lecture from which we have already quoted in the Introduction and at the beginning of this section. There is a passage in it that one can only feel augurs deep tragedy for the human race. The war was ending and peace lay ahead. Let us picture ourselves in that situation, listening to the following words.

> What I was really trying to do in *The Philosophy of Freedom* was to locate freedom empirically and thus put it on a solidly scientific basis. The word freedom is the only one that can ring true in this period we live in, and if freedom were understood in the sense I meant, there would be quite a different tone to the talk going on all over the world today about how to arrange things. We talk about all sorts of other matters these days. We talk of peace based on rights or justice, of peace based on force, etc. But we are just using slogans, because rights and force are words that no longer have any connection with their original meaning. "Rights" is a completely mixed-up concept nowadays. Freedom is the only cause that, had our contemporaries adopted it, could have given them basic motivation and some grasp of the facts. If, instead of resorting to slogans like peace with justice and an imposed peace, we were to talk of peace based on freedom, then we would hear resounding through the world the word that could give people some certainty in this consciousness soul period.

How do things stand now, half a century later? "Freedom" too has now become a slogan, just as "peace" has. Both the East and the West misuse the terms, even though they attach different meanings to them. The time will come when we have to say that they could not achieve peace for lack of understanding freedom.

That states the case fairly for anyone who can recognize the truth of Steiner's "first axiom of the social life": "No ideas are needed for wars and revolutions, but ideas are essential to achieving peace."

The ideas of the West are illustrated above by specimens of Wilson's thinking. They are based on the unexpressed view that man is a creature of soul and body. The pseudo-ideas to which Marx has led the East and which it is putting into practice have compelling power, and this is being applied with iron consequence. From that angle, man is nothing but a body.

And in 1918, at the very moment when these two worlds of ideas stood facing one another and Central Europe's lack of any smallest resource of ideas was frighteningly apparent, the second edition of *The Philosophy of Freedom* was brought out! It broke down the door through which the Central European portion of humanity might have advanced to creative ideas in every area of life. That would have been a blessing for both East and West.

A year later, *The Threefold Social Order* [6] followed the new edition of *The Philosophy of Freedom* into print. The book was intended to provide a remedy for the social chaos in which mankind is still living. But only a thinking such as *The Philosophy of Freedom* sought to inculcate could have understood it.

CHAPTER X

The Book as a Training Manual

The workmen were told that "the very first requirement for entering the spiritual world is to learn to think independently" (cf. Chapter 3), and Steiner points out that *The Philosophy of Freedom* is not only a product of independent thinking, but a schooling for it. The following section will concentrate on exploring that facet of the book.

On clairvoyance

We read in *The Occult Significance of the Bhagavad Gita*[1] that

nobody could really develop genuine clairvoyance unless he already possessed a tiny bit of it. If it were true, as is generally thought, that people are not clairvoyant to begin with, they would never be able to become so. Just as alchemists believed that one had to start with a little gold if one wanted to produce it in quantity, so one has to start with a little clairvoyance in order to be able to go on and build up an unlimited clairvoyant capacity.

Now you could set up a pair of alternatives and say, "So, then, you believe that we are already clairvoyant, even if only to the tiniest degree, or alternatively, that those of us who are not clairvoyant can never become so? The point is, you see, that the first alternative states the fact correctly. There is really not a single one among you who does not have that tiny bit to start with, whether or not you are conscious of it. You all have it. Not one of you is in bad case, for you all possess some degree of clairvoyance. What is it exactly? It is something not usually thought of and prized as clairvoyance.

Forgive me a rather crude comparison. If a hen finds a pearl lying by the roadside, it doesn't value it particularly. Most people of our time are like such hens. They don't value a pearl lying in plain sight; they value something else, namely, their mental images. Nobody could think abstractly and have real thoughts and ideas if he were not clairvoyant. Ordinary thoughts and ideas have always contained the pearl of clairvoyance. All such thoughts and ideas owe their origin to the very same process that generates the loftiest faculties, and it is of the utmost importance to realize that the first stage of clairvoyance is actually something perfectly commonplace. We just need to recognize the supersensible nature of concepts and ideas to get clear on the fact that they come to us from supersensible worlds. This puts them in the right perspective. When I tell you about the spirits of the higher hierarchies, from seraphim, cherubim and thrones down to archangels and angels, I am describing beings who have to speak to human souls from higher worlds, and it is these worlds from which our souls derive ideas and concepts. They come to us not from the world of the senses but from higher worlds.

When a man of the eighteenth century said, "Embolden yourself, O man, to make use of your powers of reason," these were considered the words of a great enlightener. Today a still greater challenge must ring out, and that is, "Embolden yourself, O man, to recognize your concepts and ideas as the first stage of clairvoyance!"

What I have just said was stated publicly many years ago in my books *Truth and Science* and *The Philosophy of Freedom*, where I showed that man's ideas are derived from supersensible insight. People didn't understand this at the time, and no wonder, since they were of the company of those whom I have described as—well, as hens.

These passages were taken from a lecture dealing with the Bhagavad Gita, an ancient scripture of the loftiest spirituality. The following quotation comes from "Das technische Zeitalter, *Die Philosophie der Freiheit* und die neue Christus-Erkenntnis," a lecture in which the same theme is handled from the most contemporary angle imaginable:[2]

This phase of evolution, in which man looks upon nature as something quite outside him, had to come for the sake of freedom. That was why those who conducted the older mysteries had to tell themselves that they would not always be able to give people what instinctive clairvoyance had made it possible for them to understand, for that would be to render them unfree. Mankind would have to be subjected to a way of knowledge that, while it would not provide any stimulation for the inner man, would constitute a source of concepts about the outer world. Human beings would restrict their knowledge

79

to learning about external things, thus educating themselves to freedom in their inner motivation.

These were the facts confronting me with utmost urgency as I felt impelled to write, first, the three preparatory books, and then my *Philosophy of Freedom*. The problem basic to the writing of the latter was the following. What we had to face clearly was the fact that we live in an age of technology. If we are not to go doddering on in an unprofessional way perpetuating trends of a bygone era, clinging to what remains of the old instinctive views of the world preserved in religious confessions and the like, our only recourse is to take our stand on technical thinking about the world, thinking that cannot reach beyond the mechanical. We relate to this world of ours as though it were some huge machine, some vast chemical process. If we want to regain the spirit, we are simply going to have to make a radical break with the mysticism that has come down to us from an earlier day and look for the spirit instead in the de-spiritualized, mechanical world that modern science has bequeathed to us.... We have to picture the situation in earlier times one in which man did look out into the world. But he also had an inner experience of what his dreaming, instinctive clairvoyance conveyed to him. He related this inner content to what he saw around him, and therefore perceived the surrounding world suffused with spirit. He saw every living thing governed by elementals or by higher beings, because his own inner make-up conditioned him to bring that kind of perception to it.

The man of modern times for whom I wrote my *Philosophy of Freedom* in the early 1890's puts nothing of himself into his perception of the world around him; he simply studies the laws that are at work in that world, laws that can also be embodied in his technological constructions. But moral impulses are not to be found there; such a course leads only to the establishing of natural laws.... Men of earlier times were still interrelated with the world around them, so that they were able to derive moral impulses from stones and animals and plants, for all these things housed divine-spiritual beings. There is nothing left of any such content in the laws of nature. All that can be found in them now is what is used to make machines and mechanisms....

What, then, was this mission that devolved upon *The Philosophy of Freedom*? It was to show that if man, divorced as he is from nature, can no longer derive moral impulses from that quarter because his senses convey nothing more than natural laws, then he can no longer stay shut up within himself; he must get outside himself.

So I had to describe the first going beyond oneself, in which a person leaves his body. This first going beyond oneself takes place in pure thinking, as described in my *Philosophy of Freedom*. It is no longer a case of a person's instinctive clairvoyance reaching out into things; he leaves his body entirely and transports himself into the outer world. What does he have there? As he thus exercises the very first and subtlest function of clairvoyance he comes into possession of moral intuitions, moral fantasy. He departs from the ground of himself to discover the spirit in this first realm, the moral realm, within the sphere of technology, for the spirit is nonetheless to be found there.

People have simply not realized that the first level of clairvoyance is the one dealt with in *The Philosophy of Freedom*. They still pictured clairvoyance submerged in an unclear, unfamiliar world, whereas it was just exactly the familiar that this book sought to convey: the thinking that no longer clings to the material but comes to an understanding of its own nature and grasps the world in pure spirituality, in the purest spirituality.

This led to *The Philosophy of Freedom* being considered overweighted on the thought side by the mystics. It contained too many thoughts for people of their stripe. Others in turn—the rationalists, the scientists, the philosophers, the men of their time—were also unable to do anything with it because it led into an area, the area of vision, that they did not want to enter. They wanted to stick to merely external observation even in the field of philosophy. In its whole approach, *The Philosophy of Freedom* thus met all the requirements that modern humanity was simply charged with meeting.

The book's educational aspect

There is a lecture, one of a series of public addresses delivered in Berlin in 1910, entitled "Wie erlangt man Erkenntnis der geistigen Welt?"[3] It gives the clearest possible description of *The Philosophy of Freedom* as a training manual:

81

It is exceedingly important that the spiritual investigator intent on entering the spiritual world take what for other people is a means of achieving insight or of attaining a goal simply as training, as inner soul training. Let me give you an example. Years ago I wrote a book, *The Philosophy of Freedom*. This book is conceived quite differently than are other philosophical works of the present. The content of the latter is more or less intended to convey their authors' views on how the world looks or how it should be made to look. That is not the primary purpose of my book. It is rather meant to serve as thought training for those who entertain the ideas in it, training in the sense that the special way of both thinking and entertaining these thoughts is such as to bring the soul life of the reader into motion in somewhat the way, if I may be allowed the comparison, that gymnasts exercise their limbs. What otherwise remains a mere means of acquiring knowledge becomes, in my book, a way of also giving oneself a soul and spiritual training. That is exceedingly important. The book is therefore not too much concerned with whether this or that point can be argued, whether something is meant this way or that, but rather with providing a chance for thoughts that belong to an organic whole to school our souls and bring us a little further forward. This, of course, provokes many present-day philosophers who do not think of philosophy as a means of furthering human progress; they would rather see people sticking to the normal capacity for knowledge they were born with.

Here the concept of a thought "organism" replaces that of a thought "work of art." But in this case they are one and the same thing, since a thought work of art is alive and living, and therefore, like all living things, an organism.

The passages quoted below are taken from a lecture delivered in Berlin in 1905, called "Ursprung und Ziel des Menschen":[4]

Now I attempted in *The Philosophy of Freedom*, a book written a few years ago, to give a picture of the gradual educating, the purifying of man for an ascent from the level of the soul to that of the spirit. What I have just been talking about can be found in that book, expressed in the terminology of western philosophy. You will find the evolution from kama to manas described there. I referred to ahankara as "the ego," to manas as "higher thinking," and to buddhi as "moral fantasy." These are all just different terms for the same things. This gives us an idea of man's constitution as a soul and spirit, and this soul-spiritual aspect is housed and embodied in what external natural science explores and describes—a physical body that is like a sheath around it.

A similar comment was made during a discussion period following a lecture at the Technical College in Stuttgart in 1920: "You will find, as regards a free concept of man, that I tried in my *Philosophy of Freedom* to show man gradually progressing to a certain stage by developing his thinking; from there, a further step leads over from discursive thinking to a thinking that is like a beholding as well."

This motif reaches an ultimate peak in a passage from Steiner's cycle of lectures on the Gospel of St. John:[5]

Catharsis is an ancient term for the purifying of the astral body by means of meditation and concentration exercises. Catharsis, or purification, serves the purpose of ridding the astral body of any elements that keep it from being properly and harmoniously organized, so that higher organs can develop in it. It is endowed with the potential for these higher organs; all one has to do is clear the way for the forces that are inherent in it.

We spoke of the possibility of bringing about catharsis by a great variety of methods. A person has gone a long way toward achieving it if, for example, he has taken in and experienced the content of my *Philosophy of Freedom* with such inner participation that he has the feeling, "Yes, the book was a stimulus, but now I can reproduce the thoughts it contained by my own effort." If a reader takes the book as it was meant and relates to it in the way a virtuoso playing a composition on the piano relates to its composer, reproducing the whole piece out of himself—in the composer's sense, naturally—the book's organically evolved thought sequence will bring about a high degree of catharsis in him. For in the case of a book like this, the important thing is so to organize the thoughts it contains that they take effect. With many other books it doesn't make a great deal of difference if one shifts the sequence, putting this thing first and that one later. But in the case of *The Philosophy of Freedom* that is impossible. It would be just as unthinkable to put page 150 fifty pages earlier as it would be to put a dog's hind legs where the front ones belong. The book is a living organism, and to work one's way through the thoughts it contains is to undergo an inner training. A person to whom this has not happened as a result of his study need not conclude that what I am saying is incorrect, but rather that he has not read it correctly or worked hard and thoroughly enough.

In a lecture on Swedenborg[6] the demands made on the reader by *The Philosophy of Freedom* are sharply outlined:

> For years now, a fairly large number of people have been reading my *Philosophy of Freedom*, a work of pure thought. It came out in the early nineties. It would be interesting if someone were to take the trouble to count how many people in our movement now engaged in studying this book would have read it for its own sake back in those days, knowing nothing about me or about our movement. It would be interesting to discover how many would have read it at that time and how many would have said, "Well, I can't get through this tangle of thought; it doesn't mean a thing."
>
> This makes you realize how many people read this work of thought for purely personal reasons, for only those who would have read it without knowing me can be said to read it for impersonal reasons. We must look at the matter quite drily and objectively. On the physical plane people have a horror of anything that appears abstract....

But the important thing here is that a person must have enough good will and striving to reach the point of thinking, to achieve a thinking free of emotion, free of those emotions we are always running across in life. For example, a person who has not yet developed pure thinking may take pleasure in *The Philosophy of Freedom* just because his feeling inclines him to a rather spiritual view of things. But he will only have the right attitude toward the book if he accepts what lives in it because of the way the thoughts it contains grow out of and support one another...When a person really arrives at an ability to grasp pure thought, to let a sequence of pure thoughts live in his soul, then his personal mood and his ego are left out of the picture. That accounts too for the rigorousness one senses upon achieving pure thinking. One can't go on bending and twisting it to one's subjective will. It is impossible to shape a thought sequence any differently than it appears in *The Philosophy of Freedom*. One cannot hew it to suit one's taste; one just has to let it do its own growing in one's being.

One's ego is really not involved; thinking itself thinks. But this thinking matures only by reason of the fact that something else replaces the ego content that one has emptied out. The soul content of spiritual beings of the higher hierarchies has to enter this free thinking and take the place of our own. And if you succeed in gradually getting rid of the subjectivity in your thinking, a thinking teeming with emotions merely threaded through by all kinds of concepts, then the divine content enters into it. It can flow in. And then your thinking receives its content from above.

The role played by the book
in the Rosicrucian and Anthroposophical schooling

In lectures given in 1906 and 1907, one comes across a series of similar, indeed almost identical passages that we will quote here in chronological sequence. First, from the lecture, "Der Erkenntnispfad und seine Stufen":[7]

In a Rosicrucian training, the development of clear, logical thinking is looked upon as basic. Every trace of confused or prejudiced thinking has to be eliminated. The world order is approached from a very wide angle. And the best preparation for this is to study the most elementary teachings of spiritual science. A thoughtful concern with these basic matters purifies and orders the thinking process and readies the student for a mature approach to higher truths. Most of the thinking people do is chaotic. The great facts of planetary evolution orient thinking and bring it into orderly patterns. In the Rosicrucian training this is called *study*, and that is why the teacher tells his pupil that he must think his way into the elementary teachings about the human entelechy, the earth, the root races. The whole range of elementary spiritual science as it is taught today is the best preparation for the ordinary person. But those who want to enter more deeply into a training of their soul faculties are advised to study such books as *Truth and Science* and *The Philosophy of Freedom*, for they were written for the express purpose of disciplining thinking, without any mention of theosophy. Anyone who wishes to apply a strenuous and logical training of thought to further pursuit of occult development does well to subject his mind to the soul-spiritual 'gymnastics' which these books call for. This provides him with the foundation on which Rosicrucian schooling builds.

In the following year (1907), Steiner gave a lecture at the Munich Conference entitled "The Initiation of the Rosicrucians"[8] in which he said,

> When Rosicrucians use the word "study" they do not mean it in the usual sense. The Rosicrucian meaning conveyed rather "living in pure thought." It is no easy matter to grasp what this means. No other than Hegel spent his entire life trying to make the Germans understand what "living in pure thought" means, and his contributions to their enlightenment were forgotten ten years after he had died. We have not advanced far enough today to regain the ground lost in understanding Hegel, but one way of furthering that would be to show what it means to live in pure thoughts, thoughts unrelated to sense experience. Latter-day philosophers such as Eduard von Hartmann deny absolutely that we can have any thoughts uninfluenced by the senses. In their view, experience derived from sources other than the senses cannot be real. If they were right, we would have no such thing as mathematics. The Gnostics called the life of the spirit "mathesis,' not because they conceived it as mathematical, but because its higher levels are reached by a pure thinking and cognition comparable to the sense-free thinking of mathematics where it deals with forms. I tried to write a book—my *Philosophy of Freedom*—for people wanting to develop sense-free thinking. It is not a personal sort of work, but something that grew like an organism. It is a thought organism, intended as guidance for what the Rosicrucians called "study."

A few days later, Steiner continued discussing the same theme, always with a slightly different nuance, in the Munich lecture series, *The Theosophy of the Rosicrucians*.[9] In lecture 14 we find the following passages:

> Rosicrucian theosophy is supersensible knowledge of this kind, and its study comprises the first stage of Rosicrucian training. My lecturing on theosophy is done not for any external reasons, but in support of the first stage of Rosicrucian initiation.
> People probably often think that it is unnecessary to discuss the make-up of the human entelechy, the evolution of mankind, or the

various planetary stages. They would prefer having beautiful feelings to doing serious study. But no matter how many beautiful feelings the soul entertains, these cannot of themselves lift the soul into higher worlds. Rosicrucian theosophy is not intent upon stimulating feeling; rather does it seek to attune feeling properly by presenting the tremendous facts about the spiritual worlds.... The Rosicrucian lets cosmic facts speak, for that is the most impersonal way that he can teach. It doesn't make the slightest difference who the lecturer is, for you should not be affected by a personality, but by the facts of cosmic evolution about which he is speaking. That is why, in the Rosicrucian schooling, any show of reverence for the teacher is out of place. The teacher is not looking for it; he doesn't need it. His desire is to tell his pupils about things in no way dependent upon his existence.

A person desirous of entering the higher worlds must accustom himself to the kind of thinking in which each next thought grows out of the preceding one. That is the thinking developed in my *Philosophy of Freedom* and in *Truth and Science*. These books are not written in a way that allows arbitrary placement of a thought. They developed as an organism grows, one thought evolving from another. They were not influenced by their author's personality. He let himself be guided by what the thoughts they contained produced as the fruit of their own activity and were structured accordingly.

That same year the same motif is stressed again, almost identically phrased, in the lecture "Wer sind die Rosenkreuzer?"[10]

The Philosophy of Freedom was assigned the same role in anthroposophical schooling that Steiner speaks of its playing in the Rosicrucian training. In the Introduction to the third edition of the book *Theosophy* we read: "If a person prefers to pursue on some other path, the truths presented here, he will find one offered in *The Philosophy of Freedom*. The two books head in their different ways for the selfsame goal. Neither one is vital to a grasp of the other, though some readers certainly benefit from reading both." If one pursues this lead, one finds much of the material *Theosophy* presents from the standpoint of supersensible vision set forth in *The Philosophy of Freedom* in purely philosophical terms.

An Outline of Occult Science comments more comprehensively. The passage is to be found in the Introduction, where it takes up the theme of esoteric schooling:

> The path leading through acquaintanceship with spiritual-scientific truths to sense-free thinking is completely reliable. But there is another even more dependable and, above all, more exact, though for some people it may prove more difficult. It is described in my books, *The Theory of Knowledge Based on the Goethean World Conception* and *The Philosophy of Freedom*. These books point out what human thought achieves when thinking becomes absorbed in self-activity instead of working on impressions of the physical sense world. This is pure thinking in action, resembling a being alive in itself, instead of the kind of thinking given over to merely reviewing a person's past experiences.
>
> Neither of the books referred to makes any mention of spiritual-scientific matters. But both demonstrate that pure, self-active thinking can indeed produce information about the world and life and man. These writings occupy an important place midway between knowledge of the sense world and knowledge of the spirit. They contribute what thought can attain to when it rises above the level of sense observation but stops short of embarking on spiritual research. A person who allows these books to work upon his entire being is already experiencing the spiritual world, although he perceives it only as a world of thought. He is travelling a sure path when he lets this in-between stage act upon him, and that can result in his developing a feeling for the higher world that will go on yielding him the finest harvest from that time forward.

The book's relationship to science
and to the various levels of higher knowledge

We now come to a period that saw new elements playing into the anthroposophical movement as the result of young scientists bringing their training into it with them and wanting to build bridges between the movement and their scientific fields. A whole series of most important lecture cycles followed. One such was *Anthroposophie, ihre Erkenntniswurzeln und Lebensfrüchte.* [11] Not only does it show how the cognitive foundation of anthroposophy is to be found in *The Philosophy of Freedom*; it also points out the fact that this book helps one make the transition from moral intuition to cosmic intuition. The basic thought here is that Goetheanism's province is the pole of matter, whereas *The Philosophy of Freedom* explores the consciousness pole, a foundation from which one can advance to an understanding of higher levels of consciousness. We read in Lecture 6:

> ...If one wants to describe what a human being is, one can do so in a philosophical approach to freedom. In that approach, however, one is restricted to the area of intuitive experience to explain human action. If one is looking for a cosmic equivalent of this philosophical approach to freedom, one has to extend the restricted area dealt with there to include all the levels of cognition: the material, the imaginative, the inspirational, the intuitive.
>
> Systematically speaking, imagination and inspiration belong between the first half of my *Philosophy of Freedom*, where I demonstrated the reality of objective cognition, and the second half, where, in the chapter on "moral fantasy," I develop the subject of moral intuition. At the time when I was working on the book, this fact could only be hinted at....

And we read at the end of the same lecture: "Such is the connection of all maturely worked out anthroposophical knowledge with its seed-form as laid down in *The Philosophy of Freedom*. One must, of course, have some perception of the fact that anthroposophy is a living organism and has to make its appearance in seed-form before it can go on to the leaf stage and other further developments."

Grenzen der Naturerkenntniss [12] is the other lecture cycle with a bearing on the theme under study here. This course too goes into the polarity of matter and consciousness in connection with a discussion of Dubois-Reymond's "Ignorabimus" speech, illustrating the problem at hand of Hegel's pupils, Marx and Stirner. It leads to the conclusion that Goetheanism provides the proper approach to matter, while *The Philosophy of Freedom* attempts it for the consciousness pole. Lecture 4 in this series goes fully into *The Philosophy of Freedom*, emphasizing again and again that the book presents "results of psychic observation," not speculation. This lecture goes on to trace the transition to higher levels of consciousness in concrete detail. One is strongly tempted to reproduce it here in its entirety. But since it can be read in the above-mentioned cycle, we omit it here in favor of saving space for considerable portions of a lecture of October 3, 1920 [13] that followed close upon the cycle, *Grenzen der Naturerkenntniss*. This lecture goes once again into all the themes under discussion above, and at the end it points to an evolutionary aspect, that is, the development that will be brought about in finding a transition from the rhythm of breathing to rhythmic interchange between perceiving and thinking.

In my book *Knowledge of the Higher Worlds* [14] I have described a reliable method of gaining entry into spiritual realms. But it is one intended for quite general use.... The one I am about to describe today is more particularly for the scientist. Experience has taught me, however, that one prerequisite for a scientist following the path of knowledge is the study of what has been presented in my *Philosophy of Freedom*. The book was not written with the purpose most books serve, namely, to acquaint the reader with the subject matter they contain.... My *Philosophy of Freedom* is not really meant to do that. That is the reason why it is not exactly popular with people who read a book for information only. It was intended to involve the reader, page by page, in the actual activity of thinking, to serve merely as a score read with inner thought activity as the reader advances on his own from thought to thought. The book constantly looks to the reader to cooperate in thinking, and it also counts on *what develops in his soul* as a result of his cooperating. A person has not read this *Philosophy of Freedom* properly unless, after working his own way through it, he can say that he has grown out of his ordinary thought habits into sense-free thinking.

The strange thing is that most western philosophers deny any reality whatsoever to the very soul element that work on *The Philosophy of Freedom* was intended to develop....

Their denying this is due, in the last analysis, to the fact that philosophers have never been willing to distinguish between analytical and empirical methodology.

When you get right down to it, there can be no such thing as philosophizing without first grasping at least the spirit of mathematical thinking.... Many philosophers deny that there is any such thing as the very capacity I wanted people to develop as a result of studying *The Philosophy of Freedom* ....

I assumed, to begin with, that the reader would have worked his way through *The Philosophy of Freedom* in an ordinary state of consciousness. After that one is well-prepared ... to go on and develop imagination.... When one has done this, something strange happens. One notices something at the proper moment. I have been assuming that a reader has already worked his way in thought through *The Philosophy of Freedom*. Then he puts it aside and goes on to travel the path of contemplation, of meditation.... While this is going on, the thought-work he did on *The Philosophy of Freedom* is being transformed into something quite different. What this *Philosophy of Freedom* enabled him to experience as pure thinking ... now becomes something entirely different. It becomes more richly saturated with content, and while, on the one hand, he has been making his way into greater depths of imagination on the inner path, what he achieved in thought-work on *The Philosophy of Freedom* has progressed beyond the point it had reached in his ordinary consciousness.... *What was previously pure thought has become inspiration.*

Imagination has been developed; pure thinking has become inspiration. As we advance along this path, we arrive at a point where we can keep separate two different things to which we have attained as we travelled these two roads, routes between which we need to distinguish with the greatest clarity. One is the inspiration that has developed from pure thinking, the life that began as pure thought and has now been raised to the level of inspired thinking. The other is what we experience as the states of balance, life and motion. Now we can relate the two ways of experiencing, uniting the outer one with the inner. *Combining imagination and inspiration, we arrive again at intuition.*

What is the perceptive process in reality? It is actually nothing but modified in-breathing. When we breathe in air, this air presses against the diaphragm, against the whole organism. The fluid in which the brain floats is forced upward through the spinal canal toward the brain. A connection is set up between in-breathing and the brain's activity, and this aspect of the in-breathing process thus specialized in the brain works in sense activity as perception. We could call perceiving one branch of the in-breathing process. Then, as we breathe out, the brain fluid goes down again and exerts pressure on the blood circulation. The falling of the brain fluid is connected with will activity, and the latter in turn with out-breathing. But a person who really studies *The Philosophy of Freedom* finds that thinking and willing merge in the achievement of pure thinking. Pure thinking is fundamentally an exercise of will. Thus there is a relationship between pure thinking and what the Oriental experienced when he breathed out. Pure thinking is related to expelling breath, exactly as perceiving is related to in-breathing. We have to go through the same process, only somewhat more inwardly, that the Oriental went through in his yoga training. Yoga focussed on regulating breathing and thus laying hold on man's eternal nature. What can Western man do instead? He can strive for a clear inner experience of *perceiving* on the one hand, of *thinking* on the other, and he can combine in active inner experiencing, the thinking and perceiving that otherwise have nothing more than an abstract, formal, inactive relationship.

These passages, considerably abbreviated here, are followed by the comprehensive statement,

And as my *Philosophy of Freedom* gave me a merely philosophic demonstration of the fact that true reality is summed up in the interaction of thinking and perceiving, it was necessary—just because *The Philosophy of Freedom* was to serve inner development—to point out by what means Western man could gain entry into the spiritual world. The Oriental says, "systole, diastole, in-breathing, out-breathing." The man of the West must say instead, "perceiving, thinking." The Oriental says, "Work on the physical breathing process." Western man says, "Work on soul-spiritual breathing in acts of knowledge in which perceiving alternates with thinking."

Here we see what an important role *The Philosophy of Freedom* has to play in the creating of a genuine understanding between East and West.

CHAPTER XI

Confrontations

The preceding section pictured what *The Philosophy of Freedom* would have meant to the world had its educational potential been realized. It may also be useful to see what sort of difficulties the book ran into at its publication.

Rosa Mayreder played the part of fairy godmother at the book's borning, but that situation was very different from the one that prevailed in the old fairy tale. There, there were twelve good fairies and only one bad one. Here, we know that there was one good fairy, but the number of those who harbored ill will toward the book may well have been a good deal larger.

Steiner felt prompted to mention some of the problems this created for him. He took the opportunity of doing so in conjunction with the publishing of the book, *Die Mystik im Auftrage des neuzeitlichen Geisteslebens und ihr Verhältnis zur modernen Weltanschauung*:

> Ten years ago I would not have dared to respond to such a request [that of Count Brockdorff to give lectures on mysticism] but that is not to say that the ideas I have been expressing were as yet unfamiliar to me, for they are all contained in *The Philosophy of Freedom*. To express them in their present form, however, and to use them as the basis of a presentation like that in this book calls for something more than complete conviction of their truth as thoughts. It requires a long intimacy such as can only be the fruit of spending many years with them. Only now, after establishing that intimacy, do I dare speak as I have in this piece of writing.
>
> A person like myself who goes his own way must be prepared to put up with a lack of understanding. But that is not so hard to bear. Misunderstanding is to be expected, considering how the critics' minds work. I look back with some amusement on a number of "critical" judgments that have been passed on me in the course of my

93

writing activity. At first, things went smoothly enough; I wrote about Goethe and related matters. What I was saying sounded to a lot of people as though my comments could perfectly well fit in with their own thought patterns. They showed this when they said that a work like Steiner's introduction to Goethe's scientific writings could be reckoned just about the best thing ever written on the subject. Later on, when I published something of my own, they found that I had grown a lot stupider. A well-meaning critic handed out the advice, "Before he goes any further in his efforts at reform and publishes his *Philosophy of Freedom*, he is strongly advised to study those two philosophers (Hume and Kant) until he understands them." Unfortunately, the critic's own understanding extends only to what he himself could get out of reading Kant and Hume, so he is really advising me not to let them stimulate me to any deeper thoughts than he has had; he will be quite satisfied to have me stop there. When my *Philosophy of Freedom* came out, I was found to be in need of the sort of criticism to which the greenest beginner is subjected. I got it, too, from a man whose only excuse for writing books was apparently that he did not understand anyone else's. He told me portentously that I would have noticed my errors if I had undertaken "deeper psychological, logical and epistemological studies," and he included a list of the books I needed to read to become as brilliant as he was: Mill, Sigwart, Wundt, Riehl, Paulsen, B. Erdmann. It was particularly gratifying to be advised by someone so impressed with his own understanding of Kant that he couldn't imagine anyone having actually read Kant and arriving at any other point of view about it than he himself had formed. So he suggested the very chapters I should read in Kant's writings to reach an understanding as profound as his.

These are typical samplings of the sort of criticism my ideas received. Taken by themselves, they are negligible. But I see them as symptomatic of the real difficulties encountered by a person writing today on matters connected with higher cognition.[1]

When the book came out, it was weighted with the heavy handicap of its anti-Kantian direction. In a lecture given when the second edition appeared and from which we have already quoted numerous passages, Steiner said, "The ethical individualism espoused by the book naturally put the entire Kantian contingent up in arms against me, for the preface of my short book, *Truth and Science,* began with the sentence, 'We must get beyond Kant.'"

He returns to this theme and handles it with considerable verve in lectures to the workmen entitled *Kant, Schopenhauer und Eduard von Hartmann.* [2]

> Now Kant wrote that great tome, *The Critique of Pure Reason . . .* and if a true philistine comes along and is handed this huge book, he smacks his lips, for a *Critique of Pure Reason* must be awfully deep, and to be reading it makes one seem like God himself. But after the introduction comes Chapter 1, "Transcendental Esthetics" . . . A person who opens my *Philosophy of Freedom* finds a simple heading like "Man and the World." What? Just "Man and the World"? . . . What commonplace stuff! But "Transcendental Esthetics"! A philistine opening such a book thinks he has really got hold of something tremendous. He doesn't bother his head over what transcendental esthetics means. He is quite content to leave it at that. "Transcendental esthetics" is a term he can roll importantly over his tongue as he pronounces it.

On another occasion, one of the workmen asked a question about *The Philosophy of Freedom.* That was the procedure for getting the lecturer launched on a topic. The question in this case loosed a further blast at Kantianism:

> Now to a written question handed me a little while ago. It says, "I have read in your *Philosophy of Freedom* that we only heal the breach that we ourselves have created between ourselves and the world when we make the world content our own thought content." The questioner read this statement in *The Philosophy of Freedom*, and he now asks, "What constitutes this world content, since everything we see exists only as a product of our thinking it?" Then he adds the comment, "Kant explains that our minds are not equipped to understand the phenomenal world underlying the world as we perceive it."

Steiner answers this with an emphatic rejection of the Kantian approach. It has been printed in *Der Mensch und die Hierarchien; Das Verlorengehen des alten Wissens.* [3] This lecture was given in 1924, thirty years after the appearance of *The Philosophy of Freedom,* but the fighting spirit that gives the book its impact and was a feature of the often-mentioned lecture delivered on the occasion of its reappearance flares up again thirty years later, undiminished. This is apparent in Steiner's comments to the workmen. Only the question-answering part of that talk will be reproduced here:

> The question has been asked, "What makes up the world-content." It must be answered as follows.... I stated in my *Philosophy of Freedom* that it is only by making the world content into our own thought content that we restore to the world the unity it lost for us in childhood. As children we saw only the sense perceptible aspects of the whole. Thought, however, is an integral part of the full reality. So we can say that a child has access to only half of what the world consists of. Only later, when we have grown up sufficiently to develop thoughts, do we have access to the thought aspect. But it is not just in *us*. We know that thoughts *are an integral part of everything*, and we treat our thoughts as part of the reality of things and use them to reconnect us with it.

This positive statement is followed by all sorts of critical remarks about Kantianism. We reproduce below an undated entry in a book of Steiner that expresses the contrast between his approach to cognition as embodied in his *Philosophy of Freedom* and that of Kant:

> Don't speak of limits to human knowledge,
> But only of limits to your own.[4]

Before quoting Steiner's answer to the workman's question after he had listened carefully to his objections, we will quote briefly from a comment made by him about the French philosopher Henri Lichtenberger with a view to his confirming what Steiner's relationship to Nietzsche had been:

> In my *Philosophy of Freedom* I expressed my conviction that the viewpoint it presents gave the same final touch to the structure of philosophy that Darwin and Haeckel had given natural science.[5] The Frenchman Henri Lichtenberger knows that it was I who sharply stressed the basic lack in Nietzsche's thought world. He says in his book, *La Philosophie de Nietzsche*, that "Rudolph Steiner is the author of *Truth and Science* and *The Philosophy of Freedom*. In the latter work he supplies an important element missing in the structure of Nietzschean theory." He stresses the fact that I show that Nietzsche's "Superman" fails to be the book it should be.[6] He thus

shows himself to be one of the few critics who demonstrate any understanding of the book.[7]

I sent my *Philosophy of Freedom*, to Eduard von Hartmann immediately upon its publication. He must have read it very carefully indeed, for he returned it to me with its margins filled from the first page to the last with extensive comment.[8]

This marked an important stage in the book's career. The "cleverest man of the nineteenth century," as Steiner once called von Hartmann, undertakes its study and fails to understand it! In the Rudolph Steiner Archives there exists a first edition copy of the book containing all of von Hartmann's comments, and Steiner has written on it in his own hand, "The entries in this volume are Eduard von Hartmann's objections, made in 1894." It might be of interest to a limited group of the book's students to make available copies with the pages of the first edition, containing von Hartmann's marginal comments, printed side by side with corresponding pages of the second edition.

Steiner gives an account of his confrontation with Eduard von Hartmann in an article, *Die Geisteswissenschaft als Anthroposophie und die zeitgenössische Erkenntnistheorie,*[9] which appeared in the magazine, *Das Reich,* edited and published by Alexander von Bernus during World War I. It is too long to reproduce here. There is, however, a short account of its essential features in a lecture given in Munich a year earlier (1916) and entitled "Die Menschenrätsel in der Philosophie und in der Geistesforschung (Anthroposophie)."[10] Steiner says there,

In 1894 I made the attempt with my *Philosophy of Freedom* to provide just such a philosophic basis on which to approach spiritual science. It presents the wide range of human standpoints, often masquerading under such strange philosophical names, in a way that leaves the reader free of attachment to any particular approach and able to let the various concepts speak for themselves, as though each were a photograph of one and the same object taken from many different angles.

Eduard von Hartmann studied this *Philosophy of Freedom* of mine very carefully indeed, and he sent me back his copy of the book with his comments in it.

I would like to read you a portion of a letter he then wrote me about

97

the book. The letter contains many weird philosophical terms, but I think you will understand what Eduard von Hartmann meant without my explaining each one to you.

The first thing he says is that the title should be "Monistic Epistemology and Ethical Individualism"...so he seems to realize instinctively that two aspects of one and the same thing were to be examined there. But he doesn't believe that they can be successfully combined. They are one living organism in the soul's life, but not to the dry-as-dust theoretical approach. That was his opinion, and others like it followed.

So Eduard von Hartmann said, "This book fails to reconcile Hume's absolute phenomenalism with the God-oriented phenomenalism of Bishop Berkeley, to reconcile immanent or subjective phenomenalism with Hegel's transcendental panlogism, or even Hegel's panlogism with Goethe's individualism. An unbridgeable abyss yawns betwen the two members of each linked pair."

And this because all of them stand there together so livingly that they carry on a conversation with each other and illumine one and the same thing from their respective sides!

Eduard von Hartmann senses that. He feels its truth and confirms it. What he doesn't realize is that it is not a question here of a thought-out, hypothetical, theoretical linking of two different things, but of an actual living experience of their oneness.[11]

So he goes on to say, "Most important, however, is the failure to see that phenomenalism leads with iron consequence to solipsism [the doctrine of oneness, of the ego as central], to absolute illusionism and agnosticism. Nothing is done to guard against this slipping into the crevasse of un-philosophy, because the danger of doing so is not even recognized."

The danger certainly is recognized! And Eduard von Hartmann is again instinctively right in using the metaphor, "slipping into the crevasse of un-philosophy." But no amount of un-philosophy or of hypotheses masquerading as philosophy is going to affect that slipping. The only thing that can prevent it is to bring real life over into that other sphere, to raise the unconscious to the level of conscious life, so that the soul's independent, objective experience can be brought back again into consciousness.

This was the most fruitful of the confrontations; its effects can be seen in the second edition. The person frequently referred to there as "a person greatly revered by the author" is Eduard von

Hartmann, and it is his objections that Steiner answers in the addenda. Thus Eduard von Hartmann became in a sense a collaborator in the new edition of the book.

Steiner was, however, already calling attention in the first edition to the divergence between his and von Hartmann's viewpoints. This occurs in the chapter, "The Value of Life." A similar reference to their differing approaches is found in a lecture of 1911, "Die verborgenen Tiefen des Seelenlebens": [12]

Eduard von Hartmann did an interesting arithmetical experiment, demonstrating in a truly ingenious way that pain and sorrow predominate in life. He took as subtrahend everything that man has to suffer in the way of grief and misery, and used for his minuend the sum total of man's joys and pleasures. When he subtracted the one from the other, he came out with a remainder of pain and sorrow. So the philosopher came, as a result of mental calculation, to the partly right conclusion that if pain and sorrow predominate, pessimism is the only justified view of life. The philosopher's reason undertook this calculation and concluded on the conscious level that the world is not a very good place to live in.

Now I showed in my *Philosophy of Freedom* that this subtraction, this piece of calculation on the part of reason, simply does not apply here. For on what does its carrying out depend, no matter whether a philosopher or the man in the street undertakes it? It is something that has to be done by the soul in consciousness. But, strange to say, conscious soul life does not arrive at a decisive judgment on the pleasure and value of going on living. Life itself proves this. No matter how many such calculations a person may make, he does not conclude from them that life is not worth living. So, even though Eduard von Hartmann's calculation is ingenious, as I said before, we see that a person making it cannot use it as a basis for real life decisions. Robert Hamerling, in his *Atomistik des Willens*, also pointed out the fact that there has to be something wrong with this calculation. For in all living creatures, man included, the desire to live outweighs its opposite, regardless of suffering. Thus a person's conclusion that life is valueless comes from some other source than this subtraction example. I showed in my *Philosophy of Freedom* that this piece of calculation has no relevance, because an entirely different calculation is going on in man's soul depths. Not subtraction; that would have to take place consciously. Instead, man's unconscious soul life does an example in division, dividing the total pleasure by the pain. You all

99

know that if we assign both pleasure and pain the value of, say, eight, subtraction leaves the value of living at zero, whereas in division the answer is one. There is always a positive quotient, not a zero. No matter how large the divisor is, so long as it isn't infinite, there is always some remnant of pleasure in living, and the division example is indeed actually carried out in hidden soul depths.

The confrontations discussed above all resulted from the appearance of the first edition. New opponents cropped up at the publishing of the second edition. Steiner felt it necessary to comment on one of them in a lecture given in November 1919. [13] He took as typical a book written by Prof. Friedrich Traub, a theologist at the University of Tübingen. He suggests that Traub probably made his criticism "on the basis of a Protestant bias of feeling" and says that "experience gives one little reason to believe that the average Protestant theologian knows much of philosophy." The book in question is called *Rudolf Steiner as Philosopher and Theosophist*; later on, Walter Johannes Stein wrote a refutation of it. Steiner discusses Traub overreaching himself in his attempt to assess Steiner as a philosopher and proves that Traub does not understand what *The Philosophy of Freedom* is all about. He quotes Traub as saying, "But then come sections that are truly obscure, and the reader is bewildered as to what they mean." Traub goes on to say that he had to weigh the possibility that Steiner's mental state might account for this. Steiner points out that if Traub had read *Truth and Science* he would have been in a better position to overcome the bewilderment caused him by *The Philosophy of Freedom.* Steiner then gets to the real core of the matter, that is, the book's completely anti-Kantian conception of the physical world. Kantianism sees the perceptible world as something complete in itself, while Steiner regards it as only half of reality, requiring completion by man in the form of concepts and ideas.

If one were to characterize what is conveyed in my book *Truth and Science* and what is then carried over...into *The Philosophy of Freedom*, it would be apparent that the thinking required as a foundation for anthroposophy has already been germinally established in philosophical form.

100

He returns to this theme in his further presentation of the facts of concern in the dispute:

So that we may say we arrive at intuitive thinking as it has been characterized in *The Philosophy ofFreedom*. Something that should be stressed in characterizing my philosophy is that this thinking that lifts into the spiritual world has already been developed....

The Protestant theologian is of course chiefly interested in "what concept I had of God at the time of writing my philosophical works. But you see, when a person writes a book he isn't trying to cover every possible subject from every imaginable angle; he is writing from the viewpoint that belongs with that particular book.There wasn't any reason at all to concern myself with theological questions about God and the universe during the time when my *Philosophy of Freedom* and various other earlier and later books were being written. It is a strange thing to fail to see that there is no way of including a personal or an impersonal God in the context of a book like *The Philosophy of Freedom.* One has to keep to the book's subject."

The man who said this is the same person who could write in the chapter entitled "The Consequences of Monism" that "to live permeated in thought in reality is simultaneously to live in God." Let us keep this statement in mind, and the more firmly it imprints itself, the more illumined do we find what Steiner had to say about *The Philosophy of Freedom* in the section to follow.

CHAPTER XII

The Book's Christian Substance

The Protestant theologian Traub asks what Steiner's thoughts about God are, but makes no mention of the Christ. Ought he to consider them equally important? How must such a theologian react to finding this chapter teeming with passages that point out the Christian substance of *The Philosophy of Freedom*? And this after being treated to such sharp correction on the score of his question about God, though he could have found answers to it in the final sentences of the preceding section.

Provided Steiner is right—and every reader has to draw his own conclusions on this score—that present-day thinking is so influenced by the Latin language that Latin actually does our thinking for us, this fact needs to be thought through in all its consequences. Does not Roman Catholicism conduct its services in that language? What of the role Latin plays in legal thinking?

Technological thinking has been the first to free itself from this compulsion. But what is doing the thinking when Latin thinks? Why, a speech element that came into being in pre-Christian times! That being the case, can we not say that a pre-Christian, pagan element is still shaping the thinking of the present? That thought forms belonging to an age that lies two milennia behind us are still influencing our era?

To weigh this is to see many present-day phenomena in a new light.

A person who looks only at the "what," not at the "how" of *The Philosophy of Freedom* will find it hard to get at the real substance of the book. He will tend to believe that he is dealing with a theory of knowledge long since out of date and superseded. The real truth is, however, that it is merely a garment clothing something quite different. [1]

The following pages quote comments by Steiner that will prove helpful in guiding readers to a conception of the "how" of *The Philosophy of Freedom*.

First, a passage from Steiner's *Course of My Life*:

> During this period, the relationship between spiritual knowledge and ordinary conceptual knowledge based on observation by the senses grew from a largely ideal experience to one in which *the whole human being* participated. Ideal experience, which can quite well serve as a carrier of truly spiritual content, was the element out of which my *Philosophy of Freedom* came to birth. Experience in which the whole human being participates opens itself to the spiritual world in a far more *real* and *living* way than the experience of ideas is capable of doing. The latter, however, does represent a stage of knowledge beyond that involved in a conceptual grasp of the sense world. Ideal cognition is not concerned with understanding the sense world, but rather with coming to know the spiritual world beyond its borders. [2]

The spiritual realm thus entered is at first featureless. But it assumes more concrete character when, a few pages later on, Steiner says:

> I cannot regard the fact that these questions occupied me as having had any great significance for me as I started out on the third phase of my life, for I had been entertaining them for a long time. What was significant, however, was the fact that my entire cognitive world, though it remained essentially unchanged as to content, was thereby roused to a vividness beyond anything my soul had previously experienced. The soul of man lives in the "Logos." The basic theme of my *Theory of Knowledge Based on Goethe's World Conception*, which I wrote in the mid-eighties, was how the outer world lives in the Logos; this also holds true of my books *Truth and Science* and *The Philosophy of Freedom*. This soul orientation was responsible for shaping the ideas that served as a means of exploring the inner depths out of which Goethe sought to illumine the phenomenological world. [3]

An entry in *The Philosophy of Freedom* dated October 19, 1918 bears on the same theme:

> Man finds in the spirit
> The path to soul illumination,

And in that light
The Word of God
That serves as his support in joy and sorrow.[4]

The first reference made was to undifferentiated spirit; the second was to the Logos revealing itself in man and nature. A small further step enables us to understand a remark—it is scarcely more than that—made in the lecture, "Exoteric and Esoteric Christianity"[5]:

> We are not really alive in the development of our intellects. We should simply sense that there is no real life in our thinking process, that we pour out our lives into empty intellectual images. One has to dispose over a considerable intensity of life to be able to feel that there is any creative life going on in the process of forming dead mental images as one enters the region in which pure thinking arrives at moral impulses, the region in which one comes to understand human freedom against a background of impulses born of pure thinking. That is what I tried to demonstrate in my *Philosophy of Freedom*. *The Philosophy of Freedom* is, in fact, a picturing of morality intended to serve as a manual for enlivening dead thoughts by making them moral impulses, for resurrecting them from the dead. In this sense there is indeed an inner content of Christianity in such a philosophy of freedom.

Steiner shows us the Christian nature of his theory of knowledge from quite a different angle in Lecture 6 of the series, *Das Karma des Materialismus*[6]:

> As a Darwinist one can just as easily be a believer as an atheist. The coin can be turned either side up. But one can never become a Christian on the basis of Darwin's teachings, nor yet on the basis of an advance in modern science, if one stops there. Something different has to enter the picture, namely, an understanding for a certain inner approach to fundamental issues. What fundamental issues am I referring to?
>
> Kant said that the way the world appears to us is conditioned by our organisms. I first broke most fundamentally and vehemently with this piece of Kantianism in my book, *Truth and Science*, and then in my *Philosophy of Freedom*. Both of these writings are based on the premise that we are not remote from reality in the concepts of the

104

world that we form within us, that on the contrary we are born into physical bodies just in order to have eyes to see the world with, ears to hear it, and so on. What our senses perceive is one half of reality, not the whole thing. I stressed the same fact in my *Riddles of Philosophy*. It is the way we are organized that makes the world in some sense what the Orientals call Maya, or illusion. As we make mental pictures of the world, we restore to it in thought what we suppressed on entering a body. That is the true relationship between fact and science. Genuine science is the completed thought of the thing perceived. On the basis of this idea: 1) that the unreality of the aspect first presented to our senses by the world is due to the way we, not the world, are made, and 2) that we restore to the world by our own effort the reality of which *our perceiving* deprived it, I call this thought a *Pauline concept in the field of cognitive theory*. For what is it if not a carrying over into the realm of philosophy the Pauline idea that man in the person of Adam entered upon an inferior experience of the world, and only comes to experience it as it really is through Christ's influence on him? Christianity can wait for philosophy and epistemology to get around to it. In any case, the important thing is not to base cognitive theory on the theological formulae in use, but on the *kind* of thinking done. So I may say that a Pauline spirit lives in the books, *Truth and Science* and *The Philosophy of Freedom*, even though they are products of a completely philosophical approach. It is possible to find a bridge from this way of philosophizing to the Christ spirit, just as one can find a bridge from natural science to the Father spirit. The natural scientific way of thinking cannot, however, find the way to Christ. Therefore, so long as Kantianism, which represents a decidedly pre-Christian standpoint, continues to be influential, philosophy will only further obscure Christianity. Philosophy will be colored by a false, distorted Christianity if Kantianism goes on flourishing as the basis of epistemology.

It may strike this or that reader as superfluous to bring up the same motif yet once again. It was approached in the previously quoted passages from the standpoint of Western natural science and epistemology. The following quote looks at the problem in its Eastern aspect. It comes from Lecture 7 of the series, *The Christ Impulse and the Development of Ego Consciousness.*[7] The preceding lectures are on the subject of the transformation of conscience.

105

What will come of conscience as it is presently developing? How does conscience manifest, looked at as a germinal element in this period through which the human race is passing? What will be the effect of the seed of conscience as it goes on growing? Why, these higher capacities that I have been describing [seeing one's future karma]. That is the important thing: believing in the evolution of the soul from incarnation to incarnation and from epoch to epoch. We learn this as we learn to understand true Christianity. There is still a great deal that we could learn from St. Paul. If you look into all the Oriental religions, including Buddhism, you will find them teaching that the outer world is Maya. It is of course Maya, but the Orient presents the fact as absolute truth. St. Paul also recognized it to be true and gave it quite sufficient emphasis. He also stressed another fact, however, namely, that man does not perceive reality when he looks out into the surrounding world. Why is this? Because he himself changed external reality into illusion on his descent into matter. It was man's own deed that made the world around him appear illusory. You may ascribe our seeing the world as illusion to the "Fall," as the Bible does, or to some other cause. Oriental religions blame man's perceiving the world as Maya on the "gods." But Paul says you should beat your own breast, for you descended into the world, dimming your outlook to the point that you do not really see forms and colors as something spiritual. Do you believe that they have independent material existence? No, they are Maya, and that is your doing! You, O man, are charged with redeeming yourself from this situation you created. You must make it good again. You descended into matter. Now you must redeem and free yourself from it, but not in a Buddhistic overcoming of the will to live. Not that way, but by perceiving earth's life in its reality. What you yourself made into Maya you must now set right again in your own being, and that you can do by receiving Christ into your soul. He will show you the outer world in its reality.

Here we have a major impulse of the West, a new trend, one that has by no means been brought to fruition in the various fields. What notice has the world taken of the fact that in one area, that of cognitive theory, an actual attempt was made to create a Pauline epistemology? This theory of knowledge could not say with Kant that "the thing in itself is beyond our knowing." It could only say, "Your organization has made it such, O man. You distort reality by being as you are. You must undertake an inner effort that will restore Maya to the true state of things, restore its spiritual reality." The mission of my book, *Truth and Science* and of *The Philosophy of Freedom* was to put cognitive theory on a Pauline basis. Both these books fit into the Pauline view of man in the Western world that was such an important goal. That is why they are so little understood, except in certain circles, for they are based on the same impulses that have come to expression in the spiritual-scientific movement. The greatest must find expression in the smallest.

There is a direct connection between these words and the following, taken from the lecture, "Das technische Zeitalter, die Philosophie der Freiheit und die neue Christus-Erkenntnis": [8]

So, on the one hand, one can incline wholly to making freedom possible while trying on the other to live the Pauline saying, "Not I, but Christ in me." Then, as man suffuses the world with the Christian impulse, it becomes possible for him to undertake transforming what would otherwise simply fall away from that divine world to which man himself actually belongs.

The forces of Ahriman, which would otherwise have worked on the earth in what had fallen away from the gods, were thus countered by the Christ force, placed on earth to work there by divine decision. Christ did not need to become free, for He is a god and remains divine even though He has experienced death. He takes on nothing of earth's nature; He lives within earth's being as a god. As a consequence of this, man now has the possibility of putting everything he possesses on freedom's side of the scale, of pursuing a path without reservation individualistic, for moral fantasy is to be found only in the individual. That is why my *Philosophy of Freedom* has been called a philosophy of individualism in the most extreme sense. It had to be such because it is also the most Christian of philosophies. So one side of the scale had to receive the full weight of what knowledge of outer nature has to offer, an element accessible to the spiritual in pure, free thinking only. That thinking can still be applied in the realm of purely technical science. On the other side of the scale we must put a true understanding of the Christ, a true understanding of the Mystery of Golgatha.

So it was a matter of course that I should try to write *The Philosophy of Freedom* to the best of my ability; obviously, one can't do a perfect job the first time around. My books, *Mysticism and Modern Thought* and *Christianity as Mystical Fact*, called attention

107

on the other hand to the Mystery of Golgatha. The two halves were simply meant to be part of one whole. But people who look at things externally and see a contradiction between the two, picture me proceeding by putting weights on one side of the scale and meat on the other, and they say, "What is this? Put everything on the same side where it belongs!" So they try to do that, but you can't balance things that way. That is how the critics of our time want it done, however.... If the soul of modern man is to relate rightly to the world's ongoing evolution, it must feel a strong impulse to freedom on the one hand, to an inner experience of the Mystery of Golgatha on the other.... My *Philosophy of Freedom* presupposes only the kind of natural scientific thinking that one would also apply to understanding a steam engine. But to understand a steam engine one has to strip off everything one is as a human being except that very last possession, one's pure thinking. We have to develop that within ourselves and then apply it to what is outside us. But it is the very same element that lives in the surrounding world of objects. So, on the one hand, we can take our stand entirely on freedom, but we have to balance this on the other side by taking our stand on the foundation of the fact of Christ.

The following comment, taken from Lecture 10 of the cycle, *Philosophie, Kosmologie und Religion*,[9] seems well suited to bringing in the theme of the Michaelic impulse:

A true understanding of the idea of destiny, pursued right into the spiritual world, cannot be based on a philosophy of determinism, but rather on a real philosophy of freedom such as I felt called upon to offer in my book of that title, written in the 1890's.

Determinism is in total conflict with impulses of Christian, Michaelic origin. Steiner goes into this aspect of the book in *Anthroposophic Leading Thoughts*[10] in passages quoted in the Introduction.

A person who allows his whole attitude and feeling to be permeated by inward contemplation of Michael's deeds and being comes to understand how to conceive a world that, while it is the work of the gods, is no longer the scene of their present manifestation and activity. As he surveys this world in a cognitive approach, he sees before him all sorts of shapes and forms that clearly reveal their divine origin, but in which, if he regards it without illusion, no actual divine life is presently discernible. And the cognitive approach is not the only

108

one to take, though it does most clearly reveal the configuration of the world surrounding man today. Feeling and exerting one's will and working hold more meaning for everyday life in a world the divine shaping of which may indeed be sensed but which can no longer be experienced as divinely quickened. Introducing morality into a world of this kind calls for the ethical impulses which I described in *The Philosophy of Freedom*.

He goes on to say,[11]

> When one contemplates Michael's present activity with spiritual vision, one is in a position to gain spiritual-scientific insight into the cosmic nature of freedom.
>
> This has *no* connection with *The Philosophy of Freedom*, which is the product of an ability on the part of purely human cognitive powers to extend themselves into the spiritual realm. It does not require intercourse with beings of a higher order as a basis for achieving its cognitive content. But one is justified in saying that *The Philosophy of Freedom* serves to prepare one for understanding facts about freedom that can then become actual experience in intercourse with Michael.

An entry in one of Rudolf Steiner's notebooks provides a suitable ending to this section and the book:

> Jah-veh rules in the hereditary element. He lives in the process whereby heredity transmits earth consciousness, giving rise to man's proneness to abstraction. Evil is generated when the abstractive capacity coupled to material existence comes into play. Then the will enters the sphere of spirits of obstruction. Jah-veh directs consciousness in sleep, but the sleeper is not conscious of his doing so. The spatial universe perceived in our waking state reveals nothing of God. The Jah-veh wisdom does not lead to knowing the divine except where it lives in the kind of love *attached to the bloodstream*. In an age when this kind of revelation is dying out, another element must enter the picture making it possible to grasp the human being *as soul and spirit. He will be understood in his soul aspect by a science of freedom, in his spiritual aspect by anthroposophy*. Modern science has brought the content of the Jah-veh revelation into realization. But the time has come when this revelation threatens to fall victim to the enemies created by it. The spirits of space want to destroy the effectiveness of the spirit that works *into* space but is not itself present there. They will not succeed if the spirit with which man-in-space is

109

endowed seeks out the spiritual that is at home in a non-spatial realm....*

---

*Published in 'Nachrichten der Rudolf Steiner Nachlassverwaltung,' No. 13; Easter 1965. The transition from the Christian to the specifically Michaelic aspect may puzzle readers unfamiliar with the material in question, though mention was made of it in the Introduction. It is well to remember that this is not a treatise on anthroposophy, but a "Monograph on The Philosophy of Freedom." It would therefore not be suitable to leave out the above. One can treat it as a remark one does not have to be concerned with or just let it stand on its own merits. Steiner's notebooks contain many samples of his efforts to ground the lightning of supersensible perceptions. For such perceptions remain meaningless for the perceiver, and even more so for the recipient of descriptions of them, if they are not brought to conceptual completion. The above notebook entry is to be taken in this sense. It is obviously intended for later use in lecturing, and for that reason transcends the limits of the theme we are discussing here. However, if one studies just the one line of the quote that goes into the difference between "anthroposophy" and "the science of freedom," it can help one to an important goal in understanding. The remainder of the quote can then perfectly well be disregarded for the moment.

Epilogue

New Year's Day 1919 stands out in my memory as a never-to-be-forgotten date. At the time, I was one of a group of prisoners housed in the barracks of the French Alpine Chasseurs at Albertville, Savoy, near Conflans, the confluence of the Isére and the Arly. Despite the fact that it was a holiday, mail was distributed. Mine brought me a copy of *The Philosophy of Freedom*. That was the fulfillment of a burning wish. I had been on leave in Hamburg half a year earlier—it must have been in June or July 1918—and was introduced there to Rudolf Steiner by my mother. Not long afterwards I was taken prisoner. One of the first letters I was permitted to write was to Dr. Steiner, asking for a copy of *The Philosophy of Freedom*. I did not know at the time that the second edition of the book was just appearing. Now it lay before me like a gift from heaven.

That was the start of a study that has never known an interruption and will never end as long as I live.

Such modest fruits of study as I have been able to garner in forty-five years of work on this book have found literary expression in several small publications.

The idea of collecting perhaps not all, but at least the most important comments Steiner made in the course of time about *The Philosophy of Freedom* had long occupied me, but it shared the fate of a good many ideas in that nothing was done about it. Only now has sufficient leisure come my way to bring this long-cherished plan to fulfillment. It could not have been accomplished so quickly had it not been for the preliminary work done by Frl. Wiesberger and generously made available to me, or for the notes collected by Frau Sophie Schmid, which she let me inspect. Other friends also provided me with references. I take this opportunity of thanking all of them most heartily.

Many a reader has certainly long been familiar with some or all of the material presented in this volume. Perhaps he too will find it stimulating to have available the collected wealth of scattered comments.

Dornach, April 1964 Otto Palmer

Notes

1 A lecture given by Dr. Steiner in Dornach, October 27, 1918, included in *Geschichtliche Symptomatologie*, Bibl. No. 185. Rudolf Steiner Nachlassverwaltung, Dornach, Switzerland, 1962, pp. 125ff. An English translation of these lectures is in preparation.

2 *The Riddles of Philosophy* by Rudolf Steiner. Anthroposophic Press, Spring Valley, New York, 1973.

3 This is merely touched on here since the editor has gone fully into the matter elsewhere. Cf. Collateral Reading.

4 *Philosophy and Anthroposophy* by Rudolf Steiner. A lecture given in Stuttgart, August 17, 1918. It was published in English as a brochure with a preface by Dr. Steiner. Anthroposophical Publishing Co., London, 1929.

5 *The Language of the Consciousness* Soul by Carl Unger. New Knowledge Books, London.

6 *An Outline of Occult Science* by Rudolf Steiner. Anthroposophic Press, Spring Valley, New York, 1972.

7 *The Theory of Knowledge Based on Goethe's World Conception* by Rudolf Steiner. Anthroposophic Press, Spring Valley, New York, 1968.

8 *Philosophy and Anthroposophy.*

9 Cf. the *Epilogue.*

10 *The Course of My Life* by Rudolf Steiner. Anthroposophic Press, Spring Valley, New York, 1970.

11 "The Initiation of the Rosicrucians," a lecture given by Rudolf Steiner in Munich, May 19, 1907. An English translation can be found in the Anthroposophic News Sheet, Vol. 16, 1948, p. 57.

12 *Geschichtliche Symptomatologie*, p. 125 ff.

Chapter I

1 *The Course of My Life*, pp. 43-44.

2 *Ibid.*, p. 51.

3 *Ibid.*, p. 103.

4 *Ibid.*, p. 174.

5 *Ibid.*, p. 118.

6 *Briefe von Rudolf Steiner*, Vol. II, No. 70. R. S. Nachlassverwaltung, Dornach, Switzerland, 1953.

7 *The Course of My Life*, pp. 219-220.

8 *Ibid.*, p. 148.

113

[9] *Soziales Verständnis aus geisteswissenschaftlicher Erkenntnis (Die geistigen Hintergründe der sozialen Frage,* Band III) by Rudolf Steiner. Bibl. No. 191. R. S. Nachlassverwaltung, 1972.

[10] *The Course of My Life,* p. 119.

[11] *Ibid.,* pp. 122-123.

[12] *Wahrspruchworte* by Rudolf Steiner. Bibl. No. 40. R. S. Nachlassverwaltung, 1965, p. 197.

[13] *The Course of My Life,* p. 187.

[14] *Briefe,* Vol. II, No. 72.

Chapter II

[1] *Soziales Verständnis,* Vol. IV, Lecture 2.

[2] *Ibid.,* p. 269 ff.

[3] *The Course of My Life,* pp. 104-105.

[4] *Ibid.,* pp. 131-132.

[5] Bibl. No. 258. R. S. Nachlassverwaltung, 1959.

[6] "Problems of Nutrition," a lecture given by Dr. Steiner in Munich, January 8, 1909. Anthroposophic Press, Spring Valley, New York, 1969. This lecture has not yet been published in German (Archive 1902a).

[7] Published in *Menschenwerden, Weltenseele und Weltengeist* by Rudolf Steiner. Bibl. No. 205. R. S. Nachlassverwaltung, 1967.

[8] Written by hand in Mme. Marie Steiner's copy of the 1918 edition of *The Philosophy of Freedom.* Reproduced in *Wahrspruchworte,* p. 112.

Chapter III

[1] *Rhythmen im Kosmos und im Menschenwesen; Wie kommt man zum Schauen der geistigen Welt?* by Rudolf Steiner. Bibl. No. 350. R. S. Nachlassverwaltung, 1962, p. 140 ff.

[2] *Der Goetheanismus, ein Menschen-Umwandlungsimpuls und Auferstehungsgedanke* by Rudolf Steiner. Bibl. No. 188. R. S. Nachlassverwaltung, 1942, p. 59.

[3] *Mystery Knowledge & Mystery Centres* by Rudolf Seiner. Rudolf Steiner Press, London, 1973.

[4] *The Philosophy of Thomas Aquinas* by Rudolf Steiner. Three lectures given at Dornach, May 22-24, 1920. Rudolf Steiner Press, London, 1932, p. 78.

Chapter IV

[1] *The Course of My Life,* p. 251.

[2] *Soziales Verständnis,* Vol. III.

[3] *Karmic Relationships* Vol. I by Rudolf Steiner. Rudolf Steiner Press, London, 1972, p. 42.

[4] Included in *Menschenwerden, Weltenseele und Weltengeist* by Rudolf Steiner. Bibl. No. 205. R. S. Nachlassverwaltung, 1967.

[5] *Geschichtliche Notwendigkeit und Freiheit* by Rudolf Steiner. Bibl. No. 179. R. S. Nachlassverwaltung, 1973. These lectures are available in English in the Anthroposophical News Sheet, Vol. 2, 1934.

[6] *Ibid.*, lecture 5.

[7] *Karmic Relationships*, pp. 49-50.

Chapter V

[1] *The Younger Generation: Educational and Spiritual Impulses for Life in the Twentieth Century* by Rudolf Steiner. Anthroposophic Press, Spring Valley, New York, 1967.

[2] *Soziales Verständnis*, Vol. I, p. 145 f.

[3] Berlin, March 5, 1922. Archive 4776, pp. 13-14.

[4] Archive 4835, p. 16.

[5] *Anthroposophie, ihre Erkenntniswurzeln und Lebensfrüchte* by Rudolf Steiner. Bibl. No. 78. R. S. Nachlassverwaltung, 1968, lecture 2.

[6] *Some Characteristics of Today* by Rudolf Steiner. A lecture given in Heidenheim, June 12, 1919. Rudolf Steiner Press, London, 1943.

[7] A lecture given in The Hague, November 3, 1922. It is to be found in English in the Anthroposophical News Sheet, Vol. 9, 1941, p. 369.

Chapter VI

[1] *Vom Menschenrätsel* by Rudolf Steiner. Bibl. No. 20. R. S. Nachlassverwaltung. 1960. Excerpts from this book are available in English under the title *The Case for Anthroposophy*. Rudolf Steiner Press, London, 1970.

[2] "*New Thinking, New Willing; The Three Phases of Anthroposophic Work*," a lecture given in Stuttgart, February 6, 1923. Included in *Awakening to Community* by Rudolf Steiner. Anthroposophic Press, Spring Valley, New York, 1975, pp. 39-45.

[3] Included in *Erdenwissen und Himmelserkenntnis* by Rudolf Steiner. Bibl. No. 221. R. S. Nachlassverwaltung, 1966. An extract of this lecture in English entitled "On the Way in Which Anthroposophy Should be Represented" was published in Anthroposophical Movement, Vol. 9, 1932, p. 29.

[4] *Ibid.*, p. 30 (in German edition).

[5] *Ibid.*, pp. 36-37 (in German edition).

[6] "Freedom and Love," a lecture by Rudolf Steiner, Dornach, December 19, 1920. Included in *The Bridge Between Universal Spirituality and the Physical Constitution of Man*. Anthroposophic Press, Spring Valley, New York, 1958.

[7] *Ibid.*, pp. 50-54.

[8] *Wahrspruchworte*

[9] An unpublished lecture given in Munich, May 1, 1918. Archive 3515.

Chapter VII

[1] A lecture given in Stuttgart, June 15, 1920. Included in *Drei Gegenwartsreden* by Rudolf Steiner. R. S. Nachlassverwaltung.

Chapter VIII

[1] *Entwicklungsgeschichtliche Unterlagen zur Bildung eines sozialen Urteils* by Rudolf Steiner. Bibl. No. 185a. R. S. Nachlassverwaltung, 1963, pp. 64-65.

[2] An essay published in *Methodische Grundlagen der Anthroposophie* by Rudolf Steiner. Bibl. No. 30. R. S. Nachlassverwaltung, 1961, p. 207.

[3] *Anthroposophie, ihre Erkenntniswurzeln und Lebensfrüchte*, p. 207.

[4] *Soziales Verständnis*, Vol. III, lecture 3, p. 35.

[5] *Entwicklungsgeschichtliche Unterlagen*, p. 52.

[6] *Ibid.*, p. 131.

[7] *Ibid.*, pp. 208-209.

[8] *Ibid.*, p. 215.   p.   215.

[9] Included in *Die soziale Grundforderung unserer Zeit* by Rudolf Steiner. Bibl. No. 186. R. S. Nachlassverwaltung, 1963, p. 176.

Chapter IX

[1] "Episodisches aus der Zeit..." included in *Geschichtliche Symptomatologie*.

[2] A lecture given in Stuttgart, June 10, 1920. Included in *Der Weg zu gesundem Denken* by Rudolf Steiner. R. S. Nachlassverwaltung, pp. 28-29.

[3] Cf. *Anthroposophie, ihre Erkenntniswurzeln und Lebensfrüchte*, lecture 2, p. 21.

[4] Ten lectures by Rudolf Steiner given in Christiania, June 2-12, 1912. Rudolf Steiner Press, London, 1964.

[5] A lecture included in *Gedankenfreiheit und soziale Kräfte* by Rudolf Steiner. Bibl. No. 333. R. S. Nachlassverwaltung, 1971.

[6] An abridged version of *Die Kernpunkte der sozialen Frage*. Anthroposophic Press, Spring Valley, New York, 1972.

Chapter X

[1] Nine lectures by Rudolf Steiner given in Helsingfors, May 28-June 5, 1913. Anthroposophic Press, Spring Valley, New York, 1968.

[2] A lecture given by Dr. Steiner in Dornach, May 7, 1922. Included in *Das menschliche Seelenleben im Zusammenhang mit der Weltentwicklung*. Verlag Zbinden, Basel, 1959, p. 67.

[3] A lecture given by Dr. Steiner in Berlin, December 15, 1910. Included in *Antworten der Geisteswissenschaft auf die grossen Fragen des Daseins*. Bibl. No. 60. R. S. Nachlassverwaltung, 1959, p. 200.

[4] A lecture given by Dr. Steiner in Berlin, February 9, 1905. Included in *Grundbegriffe der Theosophie*. Bibl. No. 53. R. S. Nachlassverwaltung, 1957, p. 145.

[5] *The Gospel of St. John* by Rudolf Steiner. A cycle of twelve lectures given at Hamburg, May 18-31, 1908. Anthroposophic Press, Spring Valley, New York, 1973, p. 174.

[6] "Schwierigkeiten des Eindringens in die geistige Welt" by Rudolf Steiner. A lecture given in Dornach, September 14, 1915. Included in *Was in der Anthroposophischen Gesellschaft vorgeht*, 16 Jahrg. 1939, No. 10, pp. 38, 41. An English translation of this lecture, "Difficulties We Encounter When Penetrating the Spiritual World," can be found in Anthroposophic News Sheet, Vol. 7, 1939, p. 62.

[7] "Der Erkenntnispfad und seine Stufen" a lecture by Rudolf Steiner given in Berlin, October 20, 1906. Published in Dornach, 1933, p. 5 ff.

[8] "The Initiation of the Rosicrucians," Anthroposophic News Sheet, Vol. 16, 1948, p. 57.

[9] *The Theosophy of the Rosicrucians* by Rudolf Steiner. Rudolf Steiner Press, London, 1966, p. 160.

[10] A lecture given in Berlin, March 14, 1907. Included in *Die Erkenntnis des Uebersinnlichen in unserer Zeit* by Rudolf Steiner. Bibl. No. 55. R. S. Nachlassverwaltung, 1959, p. 187 ff.

[11] *Anthroposophie, ihre Erkenntniswurzeln und Lebensfrüchte*, p. 17 ff.

[12] *Grenzen der Naturerkenntnis* by Rudolf Steiner. Bibl. No. 322. R. S. Nachlassverwaltung, 1969.

[13] *Ibid.*, p. 40 ff.

[14] *Knowledge of the Higher Worlds and Its Attainment* by Rudolf Steiner. Anthroposophic Press, Spring Valley, New York.

Chapter XI

[1] *Die Mystik im Auftrage des neuzeitlichen Geisteslebens und ihr Verhältnis zur modernen Weltanschauung* by Rudolf Steiner. Bibl. No. 7. R. S. Nachlassverwaltung, 1960, pp. 11-13. This work was published in English with the title *Mysticism and Modern Thought*. Rudolf Steiner Publishing Company, London, 1928.

[2] Dornach, 1952, p. 6 ff.

[3] *Ibid.*

[4] *Wahrspruchworte.*

[5] cf. Chapter 12, "Moral Fantasy."

[6] *Methodische Grundlagen der Anthroposophie* by Rudolf Steiner. Bibl. No. 30. R. S. Nachlassverwaltung, 1961, p. 200.

[7] cf. end of Chapter I.

[8] *The Course of My Life*, p. 182.

[9] *Die Geisteswissenschaft als Anthroposophie und die zeitgenössische Erkenntnistheorie* by Rudolf Steiner. An essay written in 1917. R. S. Nachlassverwaltung, 1950.

[10] A lecture given in Zurich, October 9, 1916. Published in *Die Menschenschule*, Vol. 8/9, p. 229.

[11] cf. Chapter II.

[12] Included in *Menschengeschichte im Lichte der Geistesforschung* by Rudolf Steiner. Bibl. No. 61. R. S. Nachlassverwaltung, 1961.

[13] *Soziales Verständnis*, Vol. IV, lecture 4, p. 53 ff.

Chapter XII

[1] cf. the last paragraphs of Chapter III.

[2] *The Course of My Life*, pp. 242-243.

[3] *Ibid.*, p. 253.

[4] *Wahrspruchworte*.

[5] A lecture given in Dornach, April 2, 1922. Published as a brochure, London, 1948.

[6] Included in *Menschliche und menschheitliche Entwicklungswahrheiten* by Rudolf Steiner. Bibl. No. 176. R. S. Nachlassverwaltung, 1964, p. 302.

[7] A cycle of lectures given by Dr. Steiner in Berlin in 1910. A revised English translation is being prepared for publication by the Anthroposophic Press, Spring Valley, New York.

[8] A lecture given in Dornach, May 7, 1922, included in *Das menschliche Seelenleben im Zusammenhang mit der Weltentwicklung* by Rudolf Steiner. Basel, 1959, p. 67.

[9] The so-called French Course, given in Dornach, 1922. Bibl. No. 215. R. S. Nachlassverwaltung, 1962, p. 178. An English translation is being prepared by the Anthroposophic Press, Spring Valley, New York.

[10] *Anthroposophical Leading Thoughts* by Rudolf Steiner. Rudolf Steiner Press, London, 1973, p. 86.

[11] *Ibid.*, p. 91.

A Partial Bibliography
of the Works of Rudolf Steiner
in Which He Refers to *The Philosophy of Freedom*

1893   *Briefe*, Bd. II, p. 143, 145, 148.

1894   *Briefe*, Bd. II, p. 156, 165 ff., 176, 180, 182, 185, 194, 198.

1899   *Methodische Grundlagen der Anthroposophie*, GA 1961: *Dr. H. von Schoeler, Kritik der wissenschaftlichen Erkenntnis*, p. 575; *Haeckel und seine Gegner*, p. 152, 178 ff., 198, 200; *Der Individualismus in der Philosophie*, p. 148.

1900   *Methodische Grundlagen der Anthroposophie*, GA 1961: *Goethe-Studien. Grundideen*, p. 207; *Das Chaos*, p. 440.

1901   *Die Mystik im Aufgang des neuzeitlichen Geisteslebens*, GA 1960, p. 11, 12 f., 28.

1905   February 9, Berlin: *Ursprung und Ziel des Menschen*, in *Grundbegriffe der Theosophie*, GA 1957, p. 145.

1906   October 20, Berlin: *Der Erkenntnispfad und seine Stufen*, Dornach 1933, p. 5 f.

       November 5, Munich: *Theosophie und Johannesevangelium*, lecture 7 in *Was in der Anthroposophischen Gesellschaft vorgeht*, 1945, p. 55.

1907   March 14, Berlin: *Wer sind die Rosenkreuzer?* in *Die Erkenntnis des Uebersinnlichen in unserer Zeit*, GA 1959, p. 187 f.

       May 19, Munich: *Die Einweihung des Rosenkreuzers* in *Bilder okkulter Siegel und Saulen*, Dornach 1957, p. 30 f.

       June 6, Munich: *Die Theosophie des Rosenkreuzers*, GA 1962, p. 156 ff.

1908   May 31, Hamburg: Das Johannesevangelium, GA 1962, p. 200 f.

1909   January 8, Munich: *Ernährungsfragen im Lichte der Geisteswissenschaft*, (unpublished in German; available in English with the title *Problems of Nutrition*; Archive #1902a).

1910   *Theosophie*, GA 1961, p. 12 f.

       Die Geheimwissenschaft im Umriss, GA 1961, p. 343 f.

       May 8, Berlin: *Der Christusimpuls und die Entwickelung des Ich-Bewusstseins*, GA 1961, p. 160 f.

       December 15, Berlin: *Wie erlangt man Erkenntnis der geistigen Welt?* in *Antworten der Geisteswissenschaft auf die grossen Fragen des Daseins*, GA 1959, p. 200.

1911   November 23, Berlin: *Die vergorgenen Tiefen des Seelenlebens* in *Menschengeschichte im Lichte der Geistesforschung*, GA 1962, p. 144 ff.

1912   June 12, Oslo: *Der Mensch im Lichte von Okkultismus, Theosophie und Philosophie*, GA 1956, p. 190.

1913   February 4, Berlin: *Skizze eines Liebensabrisses* in *Briefe*, Bd. I, p. 55.

       May 2, Helsingfors: *Die okkulten Grundlagen der Bhagavad-Gita*, GA 1962, p. 34 ff.

1914 *Die Rätsel der Philosophie*, Stuttgart 1955, p. 599 f.

1915 September 14, Dornach: *Schwierigkeiten des Eindrigens in die Geistige Welt* in *Was in der Anthroposophischen Gesellschaft vorgeht*, Vol. 16, 1939. No. 10, p. 38, 41.

October 19, Dornach: *Die okkulte Bewegung im 19. Jahr-hundert*, Dornach 1939, p. 90 f.

1916 *Vom Menschenrätsel*, GA 1957, p. 169.

February 1, Berlin: *Notwendigkeit und Freiheit im Weltgeschehen und im menschlichen Handeln*, GA 1960, p. 84.

October 9, Zurich: *Die Menschenrätsel in der Philosophie und in der Geistesforschung (Anthroposophie)* in *Die Menschenschule*, Vol. 36, 8/9, p. 229.

1917 *Philosophie und Anthroposophie*, GA 1965: *Die Geisteswissenschaft als Anthroposophie und die zeitgenössische Erkenntnistheorie*, p. 307.

September 4, Berlin: *Menschliche und menscheitliche Entwicklungswahrheiten. Das Karma des Materialismus*, GA 1964, p. 302.

December 11, Dornach: *Geschichtliche Notwendigkeit und Freiheit*, Dornach 1939, p. 111, 124 f., 186.

1918 April 9, Berlin: *Anthroposophische Lebensgaben* (Cycle 49), Berlin 1922, p. 14 f.

May 1, Munich: *Der übersinnliche Mensch und die Fragen der Willensfreiheit in Was in der Anthroposophischen Gesellschaft vorgeht*, Vol. 17, 1940. No. 14 ff.

October 27, Dornach: *Geschichtliche Symptomatologie; Episodische Betrachtung zum Erscheinen der Neuauflage der Philosophie der Freiheit*, Ga 1962, p. 125 ff.

November 9-24, Dornach: *Entwicklungsgeschichtliche Grundlagen zur Bildung eines sozialen Urteils*, GA 1962, p. 52, 64 f., 114, 131, 208 f., 215.

December 12, Bern: *Die soziale Grundforderung unserer Zeit. In geänderter Zeitlage*, GA 1963, p. 158.

1919 January 5, Dornach: *Der Goetheanismus, ein Menschen-Umwandlungsimpuls und Auferstehungsgedanke*, Dornach 1942, p. 58 ff.

March 16, Dornach: *Die geistigen Hintergründe der sozialen Frage*, Vol. 2, Basel 1947, p. 15.

June 12, Heidenheim: *Zur Charakteristik der Gegenwart*, Freiburg 1948, p. 12.

October 17-19, Dornach: *Die geistigen Hintergründe der sozialen Frage*, Vol. 3, Dornach 1950, p. 2, 28, 35 ff.

October 20, Basel: *Geisteswissenschaft (Anthroposophie) und die Bedingungen der Kultur der Gegenwart* (unpublished, Archive No. 3884).

November 14, 16, Dornach: *Die geistigen Hintergründe der sozialen Frage*, Vol. 4, Dornach 1951, p. 26, 58 ff.

December 19, Stuttgart: *Geisteswissenschaft, Gedankenfreiheit und soziale Kräfte* in *Die Menschenschule*, 1936: 11/12, p. 385 ff.

1920 May 24, Dornach: *Die Philosophie des Thomas von Aquino*, Dornach 1958, p. 86 ff.

June 8, Stuttgart: *Der Weg zu gesundem Denken und die Lebenslage des Gegenwartsmenschen; Geisteswissenschaft und Lebensforderungen der Gegenwart*, Vol. 6, Dornach 1950.

June 15, Stuttgart: *Fragen der Seele und Fragen des Lebens* in *Die Drei*, Vol. 5, 1925, p. 484 f., 488 ff., 491 f., 494 ff.

June 17, Stuttgart: *Aussprache in der Technischen Hochschule* (unpublished, Archive No. 4153).

September 27-October 3, Dornach: *Grenzen der Naturerkenntnis* Dornach 1939, p. 40, 43 ff., 94 ff.

December 19, Dornach: *Die Brücke zwischen der Weltgeistigkeit und dem Physischen des Menschen. Freiheit und Liebe und ihre Bedeutung für das Weltgeschehen*, Freiburg 1957, p. 67 ff.

1921 July, Dornach: *Irdische und kosmische Gesetzmässigkeiten* Dornach 1939, p. 39.

July 8, Dornach: *Der Mensch als Gedankenwesen*, Dornach 1939, p. 4, 14, 37.

July 29, Darmstadt: *Die Aufgabe der Anthroposophie gegenüber Wissenschaft und Leben in Blätter für Anthroposophie*, 1965, Vol. 7/8.

August 29 to September 6, Stuttgart: *Anthroposophie, ihre Erkenntniswurzeln und Lebensfrüchte*, Taschenbuchausgabe Stuttgart 1962, p. 17, 25 ff., 29 ff., 71, 75 ff., 85 ff.

1922 Auto-Referate: *Kosmologie, Religion und Philosophie*, GA 1956, p. 22.

March 5, Berlin: *Die Harmonisieurung von Wissenschaft, Kunst und Religion durch die Anthroposophie* (unpublished, Archive No. 4776).

April 2, Dornach: *Exoterisches und esoterisches Christentum* in *Das Sonnenmysterium und das Mysterium von Tod und Auferstehung*, GA 1963, p. 104.

May 7, Dornach: *Das technische Zeitalter, die* Philosophie der Freiheit *und die neue Christus-Erkenntnis* in *Das menschliche Seelenleben im Zusammenhang mit der Weltentwicklung*, Basel 1959, p. 67.

May 11, Leipzig: *Der Agnostizismus in der Wissenschaft und die Anthroposophie* (unpublished, Archive No. 4835, p. 16 ff., 35 f.).

September 6-15, Dornach: *Kosmologie, Religion und Philosophie*, GA 1962, p. 43, 178.

October 3-15, Stuttgart: *Geistige Wirkenskräfte im Zusammenleben von alter und junger Generation. Pädagogischer Jugendkurs.* GA 1964, p. 53, 67, 72, 77, 119, 144 f., 156.

November 3, The Hague: *Die Erkenntnis des geistigen Wesens der Welt* in *Das Goetheanum*, Vol. 20, 1941, No. 40 ff.

1923   February 3, Dornach: *Ueber die Begegnung eines Hegel-Schülers mit einem Gichtel-Schuler und Die Philosophie der Freiheit* in *Das Goetheaenum*, Vol. II, 1932, No.4 ff.

February 6, Stuttgart: *Neues Denken und neues Wollen* in *Anthroposophische Gemeinschaftsbildung*, GA 1965, p. 43, 51 ff.

June 10-17, Dornach: *Die Geschichte und die Bedingungen der anthroposophischen Bewegung im Verhältnis zur Anthroposophischen Gesellschaft*, GA 1959, p. 44, 210, 219, 221 f., 234.

June 28, Dornach: *Rhythmen im Kosmos und im Menschenwesen. Wie kommt man zum Schauen der geistigen Welt?* GA 1962, p. 145 f., 155.

November 23, Dornach: *Mysteriengestaltungen*, GA 1958, p. 9 f.

1924   *Anthroposophische Leitsätze*, GA 1962, p. 93, 101, 107, 109 ff.
February 17-24, Dornach: *Esoterische Betrachtungen karmischer Zusammenhänge*, Vol. I, GA 1964, p. 71, 4, 78, 5, 95.

May 14, Dornach: *Philosophen der Neuzeit. Der Sternenhimmel und der Zusammenhang des Menschen mit den Hierarchien.* Dornach, 1952, p. 6.

1923/25   *Mein Lebensgang*, GA 1962, p. 142 f., 149, 161 f., 167, 173, 178f., 234, 244 ff., 292 f., 323, 333, 336.

Collateral Reading

Büchenbacher, Hans:	Die Philosophie der Freiheit und die Gegenwart. Phil.-Anthr. Verlag, Dornach 1962.
Hiebel, Friedrich:	Paulus und die Erkenntnislehre der Freiheit. Geering Verlag, Basel 1959.
Kallert, Bernhardt:	Die Erkenntnistheorie Rudolf Steiners. Verlag Freies Geistesleben, Stuttgart 1960.
Leiste, Heinrich:	Von der Philosophie der Freiheit zur Christosophie. Phil.-Anthr. Verlag, 1933.
Lindenberg, Christoph:	Was heisst: Das Denken beobachten? Beiträge aus der anthroposophischen Studentenarbeit, Ostern 1963.
Palmer, Otto:	Das Erwachen des Menschen im Ich des anderen Menschen. "Blatter für Anthroposophie", November, December 1961. Quellen religiosen Lebens und Ziele menschlichen Erkennens. Verlag "Die Pforte" 1963.
Stockmeyer, E.A.K.:	Verschiedene Aufsätze in: "Die Drei", 4 and 5 Volumes 1924, 1925.
Unger, Carl:	Schriften. 3 Bände
	I: Die Autonomie des philosophischen Bewusstseins / Die Grundlehren der Anthroposophie / Zur vernunftgemässen Verarbeitung der Geisteswissenschaft Rudolf Steiners.
	II: Erkenntnistheoretische Studie / Versuch einer positiv-apologetischen Erarbeitung anthroposophischer Geisteswissenschaft / Die Notwendigkeit einer anthroposophischen Bewegung und das Werk Rudolf Steiners / Esoterisches (Wort, Gedanke, Ich — Esoterik — Erkenntnis / Sprache).
	III: Aus der Sprache der Bewusstseinsseele. Verlag Freies Geistesleben Stuttgart 1965/66.
Witzenmann, Herbert:	Verschiedene Aufsätze in: "Die Drei", 18. Jahrgang 1948.